Differentiate or Decline

Competitive Advantage & Strategy
for Private Higher Education

Brett Andrews
Robert Roller
Henry Migliore

Advance praise for *Differentiate or Decline*

Bullseye! Andrews, Roller, & Migliore offer clear, sound, and timeless insights to guide administrators through the process of understanding their unique role in the marketplace, creating a compelling organizational strategy, and effectively accomplishing the institution's most important goals. It's the education that higher education so desperately needs.

--Ben LeVan, Ph.D., President of Propel, LLC.

This book is required reading for any university leader. The book's contents provide a detailed manual for the development of a solid business plan that is critical to any university's success. Whether you have been leading for years or are in your first leadership assignment, this book has something for you. All leaders work daily to improve their skills. This book will improve both your university and your individual leadership skills. Get the book, read it, implement the contents, and watch great things happen.

--Robert M. Myers, DBA, President, Toccoa Falls College

Anyone involved in higher education knows that the paradigm has shifted. Gone are the days of growing enrollment, annual tuition hikes and no concern for competition. In the face of weak financial positions, market saturation, and decline in available students, Christian Higher Education especially needs to find another way. ***Differentiate or Decline*** takes a fresh look at these challenges by applying proven strategic management techniques in a new way. There is a lot to learn from our for-profit mentors that just might help your institution differentiate and avoid inevitable decline.

--Dr. Jeffrey Fawcett, Dean, School of Business, Grace College

Andrews and Roller make a strong case that private Christian higher education must adapt to continuing changes in market forces, the weakened fiscal viability of higher education, and the market saturation that occurs when old geographic boundaries are removed by a new model of competitive reach. They propose that habitual strategic foresight (detecting early indicators of emerging challenges) must be cultivated as a prelude to strategic planning processes. The book unpacks those processes in detail with cogent higher education examples and provides clear pathways for an institution to follow to identify its competitive advantage and value proposition. This concise book will be helpful to the leaders of any institution that wants to take a fresh look at itself in light of contemporary challenges.

--Dr. Mark Stanton, Provost, Azusa Pacific University

CONTENTS

ACKNOWLEDGMENTS

In everything we do, we stand on the shoulders of those who came before us. I want to acknowledge and hold out for acclaim two individuals without whom this book would not have been possible. First, Dr. Robert Roller. I first met Dr. Roller in his capacity as my direct supervisor from 1998 to 2003. Since then, we have worked on numerous projects together. Dr. Roller has a deep capacity to develop the leadership ability of those around him, and I am fortunate to have been one of those individuals. He is a visionary strategic thinker and a gifted administrator. I am but one of the countless individuals who owe their careers to his mentorship and friendship. As he has done so many times before, Dr. Roller's guidance and writing on this project moved it from an interesting idea to a completed project. Second, Dr. Henry Migliore. Dr. Migliore laid the foundation for the next generation of business school leadership through his role as the Founding Dean of the School of Business at Oral Roberts University. In so doing, multiple graduates of that program, including myself and Dr. Roller have gone on to successful careers as deans of their own business schools at other universities. A man of endless energies, Dr. Migliore has written widely on the subject of strategy. It is his body of written work that was the genesis for the idea of this book. His coaching and mentorship in this project is priceless.

Brett

Three of my graduate professors at Oral Roberts University—Henry Migliore, Bobby Stevens, and Rinne Martin—insisted that I do strategic management well, and I owe them thanks for sending me down the fascinating path of business strategy. Three higher education leaders invested in my leadership skills—Eugene Swearingen, Wayne Meinhart, and John Green—and I owe them thanks for having the opportunity to do strategic management in private higher education. Two of my colleagues and friends—Steven Bovee and Brett Andrews—worked side-by-side with me to develop and implement outstanding strategic plans, and I owe them much more than just thanks. Along the way, my wonderful wife, Wanda, has supported me and cheered me on, and I owe her my love.

Bob

1
WHY WRITE THIS BOOK NOW?

No Guarantee of Success

In his famous book, Paradigms, author Joel Barker introduced the world to the business applications of paradigms.[1] Barker warns his readers that when a paradigm shifts, everything goes back to zero. His meaning was that when the rules of the marketplace change, all of our organizational competencies (those activities that made a company a success in the past) become worthless. At such a point, all companies are put on a level competitive field regardless of their size, influence, or history. The future, he contends, belongs to those companies that can recognize the shifting paradigm early and move to exploit the new rules to their own advantage.

For all of the reasons mentioned above and throughout the book, we contend that we can draw an analogy from Barker's paradigm principles to the higher education industry. Paradigms

[1] Barker, J. (1993). *Paradigms: The business of discovering the future.* NY: Harper Collins Business.

1

have shifted. Prospective students, their parents, employers, and our communities all desire a different level of engagement with the university than what has been done in the past. The future will belong to those universities that know and understand their competitive advantages and can move quickly to exploit them. Since all universities carry their own strengths and weaknesses, we can't guarantee that the concepts in this book will dramatically re-shape your university. However, we can guarantee that if your university doesn't do these things, it will continue to have difficulty convincing prospective students to attend.

What's Happening Now?

It is, perhaps, a dramatic understatement to say that we live in turbulent times within the private higher education industry. When the authors began their career in higher education, the industry could rightly be classified as "recession-proof," for it had weathered recession and war, boom and bust, for decades. However, the events of the last 10 years have shattered this perception among the academy. Today, the news media is replete with stories of the financial instability of universities,[2] diminishing academic budgets forcing the closure of some programs or services, and the unfortunate closures of many of these institutions each year. Other disruptions, and they are legion, affecting higher education in general and private higher education in particular include operating deficits,

---

[2] The authors realize that institutions of higher education are referenced by multiple generic terms. The most popular of these terms are "college" "institution" and "university." For the sake of brevity and continuity, we use the term "university" or "private university" in this book to mean all private institutions, both faith-based and secular.

reduced public funding, fewer full-pay students, unbundled alternatives, a growing concern about the perceived value of a university degree, and the questioning of the amount of learning that actually takes place. Private universities that are faith-based face additional disruptions, such as differing opinions about, and consequently responses to, such issues as human sexuality, gender identity, economic and ethnic diversity, and other societal debates where there is little agreement in the church, and even less in Christ-centered universities and colleges.[3] This era of disruption is quickly becoming the norm rather than the exception. It follows, then, that we see three main categories of disruption. Each of these will be discussed in more detail in later chapters.

Fundamental Structural Changes in Market Forces. What has happened in the higher education industry since 2008 has been nothing short of a fundamental paradigm shift. Two major external forces have collided in such a way as to significantly impact the way universities position themselves competitively. First, the disruptive technology that is the internet and its ability to deliver online courses and educational content has continued to grow to the point of becoming ubiquitous. This threshold, once crossed, strips away the competitive advantage many universities relied upon for enrollment gains. Potential students have multiple choices for almost every degree program that is available in a 100 percent online format. This fact changes the strategic landscape by expanding the scope of

---

[3] Taken from Reynolds, J. & Wallace, J. (2016). Envisioning the future of Christian higher education: Leadership for embracing, engaging, and executing in a changing landscape. *Christian Higher Education*, 15:1-2, 106-114, DOI: 10.1080/15363759.2016.1107340

competitors each individual university faces. No longer are universities competing with the university across town or across the state. Students can sit at home and choose a degree program offered by any university in the world.

Second, the recession of 2008 in the United States led to a prolonged, jobless recovery. As a result, legislators in many states have reduced appropriations to higher education as way to balance state budgets. While not all private institutions participate in state appropriations, they do invest their endowment dollars. Private institutions, which historically have smaller endowments, saw the recession strip away the investment gains on those endowments which many institutions use to fund operations. Pair this fact with the fact that a prolonged, jobless recovery meant that the economy no longer provided a "pull" effect on enrollment as consumers no longer sought higher education as a panacea for their economic woes. This places the tuition-driven private institution in a tenuous competitive position.

Weak Financial Viability. Illustrating the weakened financial position of many private universities, Bain & Company, a global management consulting firm headquartered in Boston, published a detailed analysis of the financial position of thousands of American universities. The *Financially Sustainable University* project[4] shined a bright light on the liquidity crises prevalent in higher education. Among their findings were that one-third of all colleges and universities are spending more than they can afford. Still more

---

[4] http://www.bain.com/publications/articles/financially-sustainable-university.aspx

concerning was the conclusion that, "While leaders might have a sense of what needs to be done, they may not know how to achieve the required degree of change that will allow their institution not just to survive, but also thrive with a focused strategy and a sustainable financial base." In essence, the researchers at Bain were expressing their observation that, up to this point, higher education had been thought of as being a perpetually stable industry. This mentality, perpetuated for decades, has led to a bureaucratic mindset which has left many institutions exposed for what they are: inefficient bureaucratic systems that are much too slow to change in the face of new competitive realities. Bain also identified the weakened pricing position of many universities by stating, "In the past, colleges and universities tackled this problem by passing on additional costs to students and their families, or by getting more support from state and federal sources. Because those parties had the ability and the willingness to pay, they did. But the recession has left families with stagnant incomes, substantially reduced home equity, smaller nest eggs and anxiety about job security. Regardless of whether or not families are willing to pay, they are no longer able to foot the ever-increasing bill, and state and federal sources can no longer make up the difference." To survive, private universities will have to design more efficient operational structures that support a focused competitive strategy. Only by re-thinking the university's competitive position will university leadership be able to set the stage for increased enrollment and increased financial health

Market Saturation. Historically, private universities competed on many bases, none of them price. It was not uncommon to see these universities define themselves in terms of their mission, religious identity, athletic prowess, or academic rigor. These competitive advantages were effectively geographically bound and resonated well with local constituencies. Thus, a competitive strategy that worked effectively in Nashville, Tennessee would work just as well in Dallas, Texas because the competitive reach of the university's brand image was limited to the geographic region in which it was known by its constituencies. Today, universities exist and compete in an era where every customer is an online customer. Geographic limitations do not exist when all instructional and student services are available online. The result is a boundary-less strategic landscape in which many universities have similar, if not the same, value proposition. While internet delivery of the campus experience has become a necessity to attract new enrollments, these marketing actions have a cumulative effect on the market and contribute to the perception that the market is flooded with similar players. This leaves university administrators in an awkward position in attempting to answer fundamental questions, such as:

- *How then should a campus compete?*
- *Doesn't every university use a high discount rate in order to attract good students?*
- *Should we be drawn into price competition?*
- *How do we draw a clear distinction between us and the competition?*

The market for higher education is approaching what you might see in the airline industry. There are multiple corporations producing products and services and the nature of the industry rivalry tempts each company to engage in competitive activities that undermine its differentiation strategies. Described another way, universities are competing on price so as to see an increase in short-term gains, but this sacrifices the long-term profitability potential of the industry by conditioning the customer to expect a price drop in the near future. Higher education can, and should, avoid this scenario. In future chapters, we will discuss the power that a clear competitive advantage can bring to your university and why this will help your university avoid being dragged into price competition.

We Believe Private Higher Education Is Different

We believe that a private higher education experience offers a dramatically different value proposition from the education offered at a state university. In our opinion, state universities provide an educational experience centered around teaching students to think and teaching students to learn. Students who graduate from such a university will find themselves well prepared to earn a big paycheck and all the perks that come with a successful career. In contrast, most private higher education, especially those that are faith-based, teach students not only to think and to learn, but also how to live. In so doing, private universities prepare their graduates not only to be successful, but also to lead lives of eternal significance.

Being Faith-Based Is No Longer Enough.

Each of the authors has worked for a faith-based institution at some point in his career. Thus, it is that experience being brought to bear when we make the statement that simply being "Christian" or "Faith-Based" as a value proposition is, by itself, no longer sufficient as an institutional distinctive. Cultural change within the United States has lessened denominational loyalty for faith-based institutions. Further, reports indicate that the general populace shows a continual decrease in a knowledge of common grace—that general understanding that God is good regardless of whether they are believers. [5] Thus, denominational loyalty can no longer be thought of as a sustainable source of competitive advantage. Successful faith-based universities will be the ones who can effectively bridge their offerings to how millennials think and what they want from their career. Answering the question, "How is faith made manifest?" in a prospective student who is entrepreneurial, passionate about causes, and seeking flexibility[6] will become an additional challenge for faith-based institutions

If Your Campus Doesn't Change, It WILL Fail

Responding to these internal and external challenges has been difficult for universities. One university president recently wrote, "Many of my colleagues fear that for-profits will come to dominate the new emerging models and that traditional non-profit institutions will be unable to reinvent themselves in ways that will make them

---

[5] Ingraham, Christopher. (July 14, 2016). The non-religious are now the country's largest religious voting bloc. *The Washington Post.*
[6] Fenzi, F. (May 15, 2013). Survey: What millennials really want at work. *Inc.*

more effective, more sustainable, and more available to students."[7]
Unfortunately for some private universities, the last chapter of their
story has already been written with the closure of their institution. It
would not be accurate to classify every closed institution as being one
that endured problems with strategic planning and strategic
positioning. However, we have found in our personal experiences
that the lack of strategic planning, misalignment of strategic
resources, and the lack of development of a unique value proposition
is associated with institutions that suffer mediocre enrollment levels.

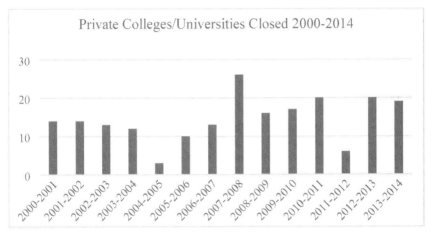

We want you, the university administrator, to realize that all
the scary stories you read about in the news are true. Universities of
all types (public and private, for-profit and non-profit) can and do
fail. It's more than simply losing a job, it's a traumatic experience for
employees and communities alike. Don't let your university be one
of the ones that populate the above chart. We want to also realize
that you CAN do something to enrich your university's future.

---

[7] LeBlanc, P. (November 10, 2014). Finding New Business Models in Unsettled
Times. *Educause Review*, 49(6).

Regardless of the position in which your university currently sits, you can chart a new course for your university that results in increased enrollments and revenues.

The Future is Bright for Those Who Plan Well

This book will be an invaluable resource to you and your team. It is the authors' belief that your university need not suffer by being reactive to the challenges in the current external environment. A private university's future can and should be determined by those who know it best—the faculty, staff, board, and administration. Planning strategically for your future will be a critical success factor for those universities that weather the current economic headwinds, for they will emerge stronger as a result. The processes outlined in this book have proven their worth in multiple institutions. In applying these principles consistently, a university will see itself thrive, not simply survive.

2
STRATEGIC FORESIGHT

We have established that these are perilous times for private higher education. We foresee that many private higher education institutions will fail over the next ten to twenty years, and that institutions who do not prepare for the future will become its victims. The golden age of private education may be past, but a new golden age may be beginning for institutions who prepare for it.

To prepare for the future, educational leaders must think deeply and strategically about what that future will look like, and then position their institutions to succeed in that future. What will higher education look like ten years from now? More specifically, what will private higher education look like? While understanding the future is challenging, asking questions about what the future may look like is essential to preparing for the future through the strategy process.

We have heard some leaders complain that peering ten years into the future is meaningless when you are in a crisis right now. But that is only partially true. Current crises do need to be dealt with, and if they are not dealt with, ten years out might be irrelevant. But dealing with a current crisis successfully while not considering the medium- and long-term future may mean that another crisis will be waiting, possibly even before the current crisis is dealt with. It's not either/or; it's both/and.

We believe that it is important, as part of the strategic planning process, to attempt to look speculatively into the future to anticipate forces that may affect a desired outcome. This process is known as strategic foresight. Strategic foresight is based on the concept of weak signals, as originally proposed by Ansoff.[8] In comparison with weak issues, some issues are easy to see, which allows the university to develop specific, timely responses; these are referred to as strong signals. Other issues are imprecise, early indications of events with significant potential impact. Since the signals of these issues are far off and imprecise, these are called weak signals. If the university is able to detect weak signals early and begin to formulate responses, it will be able to act before the signals become strong ones. Typically, if the university is operating in a turbulent environment—as we have asserted is currently true for almost all private higher education institutions—by the time a signal is strong, it is too late to craft an effective response. Detecting weak signals early and crafting effective responses quickly is one key to success. As the level of turbulence in the environment increases, strategic foresight becomes more important; so does the need for organizational processes that incorporate strategic foresight and

---

[8] For a brief explanation of Ansoffian strategy, see Kipley, D. & Jewe, R. (2014), *Effective strategic management: From analysis to implementation*, Revised ed., pp. 203-216.

individuals who understand how to think with strategic foresight.[9] As the level of turbulence in private higher education continues to increase dramatically, strategic foresight becomes essential to organizational success.

Why is strategic foresight important? What is gained by thinking speculatively about the long-term future of your segment of private higher education? For your institution to flourish in a changed future, it must be positioned for that future. If you have some idea of what the future could be, you can help shape the future. If you do not know what that future could be, the chances that you will be positioned for it are slim. Fortuitous accidents do happen, but it is not wise for the strategic future of your institution to depend on them. If you have some understanding of what the future could look like, you can attempt to align your university's capabilities and resources with that future. The process of strategic foresight provides vision into potential alternative futures which can be shaped to lead to the best possible future. It also helps jolt members of the university community out of status quo thinking. While it may be comfortable to believe that the requirements for a university to be successful have not changed, it is no longer realistic.

Ideally, strategic foresight is not a one time or even periodic event. Building strategic foresight capabilities and processes into the university's planning process is superior to one-time strategic brainstorming. However, to kick-start the strategic foresight process, an initial brainstorming process may be needed. There are many

---

[9] Maertins, A. (2016). From the perspective of capability: Identifying six roles for a successful strategic foresight process. *Strategic Change*, 25, 233.

methods that can be used for strategic foresight[10]. Here's one way to initiate the process of strategic foresight in your university.

Start by forming a strategic foresight group; whether this is referred to as a task force or committee or sub-committee depends on your university's culture and processes. The name is less important than the composition of the team. What is important is the composition of this group:

- This group should not be large; five to eight members is about right.

- One member of the group should be a skilled facilitator who understands strategic foresight processes. This might be the same person who is coordinating the strategic planning process for the university, but only if that person is open-minded and is effective as a facilitator.

- Other members of the group should be individuals who are futuristic in orientation (if your university uses the Strengths Finder assessment, just look for those who have "futuristic" in their top five strengths). They should be able to "think outside the box." The best persons are not only futuristic, but also positive. In other words, we are not recommending that you pick individuals who are unhappy and complaining about the status quo; instead, pick ones who are positive and excited about the future. Often, these are people who are a bit out of the

---

[10] For an excellent review of strategic forecasting methods, see Jackson, M. (2013). "Shaping Tomorrow's Practical Foresight Guide." Shaping Tomorrow.

mainstream of thought for the university, and that's one reason that they are good for this role.

There is some value in engaging the top leadership team of the university in the process; if so, ideally the president, vice-presidents, and deans would be involved. But limiting the process to the top leadership level would be sub-optimal. Insights about the future may come from any areas of the university or its constituents, and input into the strategic planning process tends to increase commitment to the plan. Sending out an electronic survey to all interested groups can provide helpful insights. There is no list of "right" or "wrong" questions to ask, but the following questions are good examples of the types of questions to ask.

- Ten years from now, in what ways will society have changed that could affect our future as a university?

- To succeed as a university in the future, what must we be able to do well?

- Think about where technology is likely to be in ten years. How can our university take advantage of technological advances?

- Think about how the nature of work will change over the next ten years. How can our university best prepare students for tomorrow's workplaces?

- As we look ten years into the future as a university, what is the most important strategic question that we will need to answer?

What stakeholders should you include in this survey? While clearly that is a decision for the strategic planning team, thought should be given to including individuals from the following groups:

- Faculty
- Staff
- Students
- Administrators
- Alumni
- Trustees
- Donors
- Employers of graduates

Once major stakeholder groups complete the online questionnaire, the results should be tabulated by the strategic foresight group; since these will be open-ended responses, they will need to be categorized. Breaking out the results for each of the stakeholder groups will typically be helpful. It is important, however, to not look at the responses as votes. The best insights from this activity may be individual responses that are not widely shared; remember, you are looking for weak signals, not strong ones. So every response has potential value. This is one of the reasons that it is important to have a good strategic foresight group to process this information.

Once the responses have been categorized and tabulated, the strategic foresight group should begin the process of interpreting the results. Ideally, this will take the form of scenarios of possible future events or situations that could impact the university in important ways. Often, the most important scenarios come from events that could conceivably happen but are uncomfortable to even think about, since scenarios depend on cultural change in society, the organization, or both. Here are a few examples of the types of scenarios that could emerge from the analysis:

- Five years from now, the percentage of students enrolled in online programs will begin to decline after many years of growth. More students will prefer face-to-face programs, but will still want the flexibility to move back and forth between online and face-to-face programs.

- Over the next ten years, in response to budget issues, states will gradually remove all subsidies for four-year public universities, making public universities compete with private universities without the benefit of subsidies.

- In response to concerns over perceived discrimination against LGBTQ students, federal and/or state legislation eliminates financial aid or subsidies for students enrolled in institutions with a religious mission (recent events surrounding SB1146 in California demonstrate the potential for this scenario).

These are example scenarios, not predictions. Strategic foresight is not the same as forecasting, but rather is "backcasting" from a potential future to the present. But any of these scenarios, if true, could have major impacts on the operations of your university. Considering such scenarios forces the institution to examine its mission, vision, and purpose for existence. It also helps bring into focus the competitive realities faced by the institution and the need for a sustainable competitive advantage.

As the strategic foresight team processes the information, what should emerge is a set of weak signals that are recognized as relevant to the future of the university. This information should then be conveyed to leaders throughout the organizations with a call for diagnosis and interpretation. What do these factors mean for the university? What does the university need to do to position itself vis-à-vis these potential futures? It is important in this process to avoid the temptation to fixate on a single scenario, as doing so has a high likelihood of picking the wrong scenario. Instead, it is possible to establish a number of markers that, should a particular event take place, would signal that a potential future scenario may be coming to pass. The answers to these questions must then be considered in the university's strategic planning processes as described in this book.

Inevitably, the strategic foresight process will be uncomfortable for many in the organization. It involves stepping out of our comfort zones and confronting a potentially challenging future. There will be naysayers who suggest that "wasting" time on conceptualizing an unlikely future takes away from time that could be spent on responding to known factors. Given natural tendencies toward resistance to change, such reactions are expected.

History, however, clearly shows the dangers of missing out on early weak signals. For example, Kodak went from being a dominant company in the film and camera business to bankruptcy because it missed out on the digital revolution. The early signals were there, but Kodak continued to believe that its previous competitive advantage still existed. Kodak continued to engage in incremental strategic planning processes without considering possible disruptions to its business model. The thought of digital cameras—much less cell phones—replacing film cameras was uncomfortable.

Institutions of higher education, unfortunately, do not have a much better record than Kodak. Most are unwilling to change quickly and often react far too slowly to changes in the competitive environment. This is why strategic forecasting should become an important process for any private higher education institution.

For further reading

Hammett, P. (2005, Winter). Strategic foresight: A critical leadership competency. *Leadership Advance Online.*

Jackson, M. (2013). Shaping tomorrow's practical foresight guide. *Shaping Tomorrow.*

Kim, W.C. and Mauborgne, R. (2005). Blue ocean strategy: From theory to practice. *California Management Review*, (47) 3, 105-121.

Le Blanc, P. (2014, November–December). Building new business models in unsettling times. *Educause Review*, 12–25.

Maertins, A. (2016). From the perspective of capability: Identifying six roles for a successful strategic foresight process. *Strategic Change*, 25, 223-237.

Nunes, P. and Breene, T. (2011). Reinvent your business before it's too late: Watch out for those S curves." *Harvard Business Review*, 89 (1-2), 80-87.

Olsen, E. (2011). What is futurecasting in strategic planning? *Strategic planning kit for dummies, 2nd ed.*

Reynolds, J. and Wallace, J. (2016). Envisioning the future of christian higher education: Leadership for embracing, engaging, and executing in a changing landscape. *Christian Higher Education Journal*, 15 (1-2), 106-114.

Saffo, P. (2007, July-August). Six rules for effective forecasting. *Harvard Business Review.*

3
EXTERNAL ANALYSIS

External analysis is a powerful and essential component of strategic planning. For an institution of private higher education to have an effective strategy, it must determine the intersection of its capabilities and opportunities. Capabilities depend on the strengths, weaknesses, and sources of competitive advantage of the institution; opportunities depend on external factors. This chapter focuses on how to effectively analyze the external environment to determine the available opportunities and significant threats. Two strategic tools will be presented: external environmental analysis and industry analysis. These tools interact to determine opportunities and threats; this process is shown in Figure 1. This chapter will close by considering some of the implications for private higher education, which will demonstrate how powerful and necessary external analysis is for effective strategic planning.

Figure 1. External Environmental Analysis

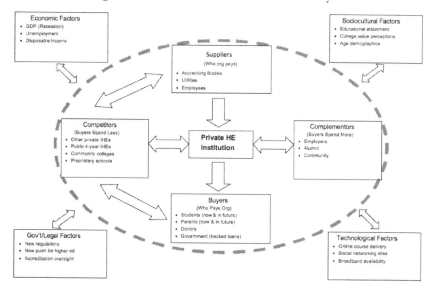

External Environmental Analysis

Analysis of the external environment is performed using a STEP analysis, with STEP standing for sociocultural, technological, economic, and political factors (if these factors are highly unfavorable, you can call it a PEST analysis instead). A STEP analysis identifies the most salient external factors facing the institution. It is not meant to be comprehensive, given that millions of factors could possibly impact the institution; rather, the focus is on those factors that are likely to impact the institution and whose impact is likely to have a positive or negative impact on the institution. Many of these factors could be common to other private IHEs, while others could be idiosyncratic.

Who should perform the STEP analysis? Generally, a subcommittee of the strategic planning committee should guide the process, but this is a great point in the strategic planning process to solicit input from institutional stakeholders, including faculty, staff, trustees, alumni, employers, and advisory boards. Stakeholders can be surveyed electronically, with responses then categorized by the subcommittee. In addition, faculty members with expertise in each area should be specifically asked for input. For example, math, science, engineering, and other technologically-oriented faculty members should provide input into technological factors. Business and economics faculty should weigh in on economic factors. Political science faculty should contribute political factors, and sociology and other liberal arts faculty members should provide sociocultural factors.

The STEP analysis subcommittee should exercise judgment in selecting the most salient factors for inclusion in the analysis, as biases of certain stakeholders or groups will become apparent. The main purpose of asking for input—other than the positive benefits of inclusion, such as buy-in—is so that important factors come to light, but the inputs should not be regarded as votes, nor should the number of respondents listing a particular factor imply that the factor is more salient. In fact, it is possible that the factors mentioned most frequently may be ones that are more likely to impact the institution but less likely to have a significant impact, and thus become minor rather than major factors.

The subcommittee should also consider perusing outside sources that can provide insights to forces impacting higher education (see the additional reading list at the end of this chapter).

For example, Grant Thornton has published an article[11] on the state of higher education for the past five years. The 2016 report lists slower growth in educational revenue, demographic changes, and technology transformation as three major categories of external forces affecting higher education. The *Chronicle of Higher Education* publishes an annual Almanac focusing on the issues affecting higher education, along with other resources, such as a webinar on the decade ahead[12].

How many factors should the subcommittee include in the STEP analysis? For each section, aim for five to seven factors. Two would be too few, and ten would be too many, but there is no exact "right" number of factors. It is likely that the number of factors included will differ for each. For a sample STEP analysis, see Table 1.

---

[11] Grant Thornton (2016). The state of higher education in 2016. Retrieved from https://www.grantthornton.com/issues/library/whitepapers/nfp/2016/SoHE -2016/State-of-higher-ed-2016-overview.aspx

[12] Weiss, M., and Selingo, J. J. (2016, October 6). 2026: The decade ahead. *The Chronicle of Higher Education*.

Table 1. STEP Analysis

Sociocultural Factors	Technological Factors
Increased concern over affordability and payoff of higher education	Traditional-age college students have grown up with smartphones, tablets, and total connectivity
The religious mission of some institutions is increasingly viewed as discriminatory, thus potentially placing the policy of hiring for mission fit in jeopardy	Lecture-capture systems, smartboards, and other classroom technologies are changing how classes are taught
Demographic trends for traditional college-age students are not favorable	Students, faculty, and staff demand unlimited broadband service
Aging population provides job opportunities in healthcare and human services	Off-campus educational centers can be more easily connected to the main campus and each other
Increased calls for accountability in higher education mean that evidence of student achievement and institutional performance are more readily available to students, families, and employers	

Economic Factors	Political Factors
Higher education tuition has increased more rapidly than family income or the CPI, making college seem less affordable	Proposals to make public college free could have drastic impacts on private higher education
Unemployment has declined, as has labor force participation, increasing the opportunities for college graduates in high-demand fields	The political war against for-profit institutions and their accreditors may provide opportunities for non-profit private IHEs
Economies of scale exist for private IHEs, making it likely that some smaller institutions will not survive or will end up merging	Increasing government regulation of higher education requires additional staffing to comply with regulations
University operating margins are being squeezed by escalating costs and increased competition	Government takeover of student loan funding is leading to additional regulation of higher education
Discount rates of private IHEs are steadily increasing	Increased local government resistance to non-profit tax exemptions for private IHEs
	Debate about the implications and limits of the religious exemption for faith-based private IHEs

Industry Analysis

Have you ever wondered why some industries—such as pharmaceuticals—demonstrate high levels of profitability year after year, while others—such as air transportation—struggle to achieve profits? The reason is that the forces affecting industry competition are different. Therefore, understanding the forces that affect the industry in which your institution operates can provide significant insights into its strategy. Michael Porter (2008) developed a model for analyzing industry competition that has become known as the Five-Forces Model, and this model can be applied to private higher education.

Porter's Five-Forces Model proposes that the favorability of an industry depends on five forces:

- Threat of new entrants
- Threat (bargaining power) of suppliers
- Threat (bargaining power) of buyers
- Threat of substitutes
- Threat (intensity) of rivalry

A detailed diagram of the model is shown in Figure 2.

Figure 2. Porter's Five-Forces Model

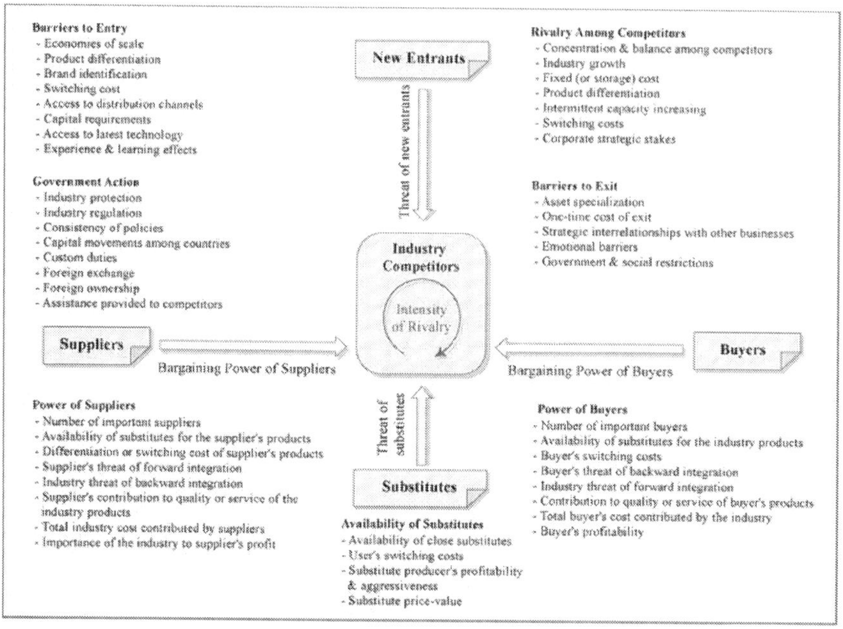

Barriers to Entry
- Economies of scale
- Product differentiation
- Brand identification
- Switching cost
- Access to distribution channels
- Capital requirements
- Access to latest technology
- Experience & learning effects

Government Action
- Industry protection
- Industry regulation
- Consistency of policies
- Capital movements among countries
- Custom duties
- Foreign exchange
- Foreign ownership
- Assistance provided to competitors

New Entrants

Threat of new entrants

Rivalry Among Competitors
- Concentration & balance among competitors
- Industry growth
- Fixed (or storage) cost
- Product differentiation
- Intermittent capacity increasing
- Switching costs
- Corporate strategic stakes

Barriers to Exit
- Asset specialization
- One-time cost of exit
- Strategic interrelationships with other businesses
- Emotional barriers
- Government & social restrictions

Industry Competitors

Intensity of Rivalry

Suppliers

Bargaining Power of Suppliers

Buyers

Bargaining Power of Buyers

Power of Suppliers
- Number of important suppliers
- Availability of substitutes for the supplier's products
- Differentiation or switching cost of supplier's products
- Supplier's threat of forward integration
- Industry threat of backward integration
- Supplier's contribution to quality or service of the industry products
- Total industry cost contributed by suppliers
- Importance of the industry to supplier's profit

Threat of substitutes

Substitutes

Availability of Substitutes
- Availability of close substitutes
- User's switching costs
- Substitute producer's profitability & aggressiveness
- Substitute price-value

Power of Buyers
- Number of important buyers
- Availability of substitutes for the industry products
- Buyer's switching costs
- Buyer's threat of backward integration
- Industry threat of forward integration
- Contribution to quality or service of buyer's products
- Total buyer's cost contributed by the industry
- Buyer's profitability

Source: strategykeys.com

One of the challenges in using the Five-Forces Model is in defining the industry to be analyzed. For example, to say that one was analyzing the "education" industry would be a very broad choice—too broad to be of much use. The "education" industry includes all educational providers at all levels, from pre-K to elementary to secondary education, to all colleges and universities, to corporate training, to on-the-job training, and much more. Defined that way, the threat of substitutes would be virtually zero, because what substitutes for education? (The answer is ignorance, but it's a very poor substitute.) And the threat of rivalry would be difficult to determine, given that elementary schools and universities are not really rivals. On the other hand, if a Baptist-affiliated institution in

Texas chose to define its industry as "Baptist universities in Texas," that would be too narrow—not that there are not a significant number of Baptist universities in Texas, but because those institutions compete with other faith-based institutions and private institutions, both within Texas and without.

The choice of industry to analyze, therefore, should be based on the institution's relevant strategic group—that group of institutions that students who consider your university also consider. This can vary widely for private IHEs. For example, some large, non-religious, privates compete not only with similar institutions, but also with large public institutions. For this group, only "national universities" might be the correct strategic group to use as the industry in the Five-Forces model. For some Christian universities, defining the industry as "Christian universities" would be appropriate. Since almost every business professor who has ever taught the capstone strategy course is familiar with the Five-Forces Model, there should be someone in your institution who can help define the industry for this analysis.

We should also note that it is possible that your institution is competing in multiple industries. For example, most private IHEs operate a "traditional" organization offering degrees on the main campus to the 18-22 core demographic, along with graduate programs offered in a traditional format. At the same time, many offer "nontraditional" degrees at remote sites and/or online. In some cases, the nontraditional programs are offered through a totally or mostly separate component of the institution. The structure of traditional or nontraditional programs is not the issue here, nor is the fact that the distinction of traditional versus nontraditional programs is blurring and becoming less relevant. What is relevant is that the traditional and nontraditional programs are typically competing in very different arenas. The set of competitors and aspirant universities is often extremely different for these two components of the institution. In other words, they are operating in different industries, and thus each industry should be defined and examined using the Five-Forces model.

Once the industry has been defined, the next step is to analyze each of the five factors. In doing so, both the level of the threat and the trend can be helpful. For example, if the threat of new entrants is low but increasing, it means that factor is becoming less favorable over time, which can be helpful to know in thinking about future strategic actions.

Several factors influence the **_threat of new entrants_** into an industry. Government action is one; in many states, the creation of a new private IHE requires state authorization. Accreditation requirements are similar in that Federal financial aid is dependent on institutional accreditation. These factors reduce the threat of entry into the private higher education industry. The threat of new entrants is also dependent on switching costs; these are costs that are incurred when a student switches from one provider to another. Credits lost in the transfer process from one institution to another are one example. The capital requirements involved in entering private higher education are another hindrance to new entrants, but this threat has been increasing due to online alternatives. Experience and learning effects, which include the process knowledge necessary to run an educational institution, are another barrier to entry. Given the ability to purchase talent in the employment market, however, this barrier can be reduced.

As we look at each of the five forces, we will provide an example analysis using the private higher education industry. In terms of the threat of new entrants, a current analysis would look show that the threat of new entrants is moderate, but increasing:

New Entrants: moderate threat, increasing (4/10)

- Economies of scale are necessary to be profitable
- Significant differentiation exists among private colleges
- Capital requirements are high
- Moderate switching costs exist
- New entrants have ready access to distribution channels
- First-mover advantages (largely reputational) exist
- Existing private colleges are not likely to retaliate against new entrants

The *threat of suppliers* is determined by several factors. The larger the number of suppliers, the lower their threat, as suppliers therefore have to compete for the business of the organizations in the industry. Supplier power is also reduced by the availability of substitutes for the supplier's products. On the other hand, if it is costly or difficult to switch from one supplier to another, the threat of suppliers increases. An example of this for private IHEs includes switching from one learning management system to another, which is a costly, lengthy process. If there is a serious chance of suppliers integrating forward—such as a textbook provider offering courses that compete with private IHEs—the threat of suppliers increases. On the other hand, if private IHEs can integrate backwards into a supplier's business, such as becoming their own textbook publisher, the threat of suppliers decreases. And if the quality of private IHEs products and services depends significantly on suppliers, the threat of suppliers increases.

To determine the threat of suppliers, consider the organizations that supply the private IHE industry. These include firms that supply products such as office supplies, furniture, lab equipment, textbooks, food, and so on. Suppliers also include organizations that provide services, such as learning management systems or institutional computing systems. And perhaps most important, suppliers include governments and accrediting bodies whose approvals are necessary for existence of the institution.

A warning is in order here, as we have found that this is a point in the analysis where users of this model frequently make errors. Sometimes users mistakenly think that suppliers refer to firms that are providing the same goods or services as those provided by whatever organization they are studying. But those are competitors, who are covered under the threat of rivalry to be discussed later. Suppliers are those organizations that supply the organizations in the industry.

For the private higher education industry, the overall threat is moderate but increasing.

Suppliers: moderate threat, increasing (6/10)

- Goods (such as office supplies, food, textbooks, etc) – Low
  - Suppliers are not highly concentrated
  - Many suppliers
  - Products are not that important to quality
  - Relatively low switching costs
- Services (such as learning management systems) – Moderate to high
  - Suppliers are highly concentrated and few in number
  - Products are relatively important to quality
  - Switching costs are high
- Accreditations and government approvals
  - Suppliers are highly concentrated
  - Few substitute suppliers of accreditation
  - High importance of accreditation
  - Accreditation is critical to success of private colleges
  - Some differentiation of accrediting bodies
  - High switching costs among accreditors
  - Low threat of forward integration by accreditors

The threat of buyers is also determined by several factors. The threat of buyers increases if there are only a few important buyers, if the buyers have access to substitutes for the industry's products or services, if the buyers' switching costs are low, if the buyers are a viable threat to integrate backward and become competitors of the industry, if the industry's products or services are relatively unimportant to the buyers, if the buyers' profitability is low, and if the industry's products or services are a relatively low percentage of the cost of the buyers' products or services. Put another way, the basic question is who needs each other more? If the buyers need the industry more, they are less of a threat.

Who are the buyers for private higher education? Three buying groups are paramount: students, parents, and employers. An analysis of the private higher education industry shows that the current threat of buyers is low, but increasing.

Buyers/Buying Groups (students, parents, and employers): low threat, increasing (3/10)

- Buyers do not have large volume
- A private college education represents a large portion of buyer costs
- Significant differentiation among private colleges
- Moderate switching costs exist
- Buyers are experiencing challenging economic times
- Little threat of backward integration by buyers
- Products/services of high importance to buyers
- Buyers have a moderate level of information

Substitutes are products or services that meet the same needs as those provided by the industry. Substitutes are not competing organizations in the same industry, but are organizations in a different industry that can meet the same needs. For example, when looking at the air transportation industry, substitutes are not other airlines, but are automobiles, trains, ships, buses, mass transit systems, etc. Similarly, when looking at the private higher education industry, the biggest substitute is public higher education or proprietary institutions. But corporate universities, trade schools, apprentice programs, and on-the-job training are also substitutes. The threat of substitutes increases when close substitutes are available, when switching costs are low, and when the aggressiveness of substituting organizations increases.

For our example of private higher education, the threat of substitutes is very high, and it is increasing.

Substitutes (public universities, proprietary institutions, delaying enrollment): very high threat, increasing (9/10)

- weak economy and online alternatives have increased the viability of substitutes
- Transferability of credit increases viability of substitutes
- Parents and students perceived less importance of an education from a private institution

The *threat of rivalry* increases when industry concentration increases, that is, when there are relatively few competitors in the industry, and when those competitors are of similar size. The threat of rivalry also increases when the industry's products or services are relatively undifferentiated and when switching costs are low. Rivalry also increases when there are barriers to exit from the industry, such as when governments or accreditors step in to keep institutions from closing.

For the private higher education industry, the threat of rivalry is moderate but increasing.

Rivalry: moderate threat, increasing (6/10)

- Moderate switching costs exist
- High fixed costs exist
- Growth rate of industry is low (approx. 1 percent)
- Significant differentiation exists among private colleges
- Capacity can be augmented in small increments
- Moderate organizational diversity among private colleges
- Strategic stakes exist, but are only moderately high
- Some exit barriers exist

To determine the overall level of threats in the industry, consider the level of threat for each of the five factors. In our example, the overall level of threat is moderate but increasing, as shown in Figure 3. Given that the threat level is moderate and going higher, it will become more difficult over time for institutions to enjoy above-average profit margins. And it will become increasingly important for institutions to effectively differentiate themselves from the competition.

Figure 3. Five-Forces Analysis for Private Higher Education

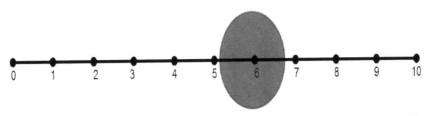

Factor	Level	Trend
Threat of New Entrants	Moderate (4)	Increasing
Threat of Suppliers	Moderate (6)	Increasing
Threat of Buyers	Low (3)	Increasing
Threat of Substitutes	Very high (9)	Increasing
Threat of Rivalry	Moderate (6)	Increasing
Overall Threat	Moderate (5.5)	Increasing

External Analysis: Implications

The purpose of external analysis is to help define the external opportunities and threats facing the organization. External analysis is a powerful and necessary tool in strategic planning. In the case of the current situation facing private higher education, the STEP analysis and Five-Forces Analysis paint a somewhat dreary picture. The STEP analysis shows that many external factors are not favorable. The Five Forces Analysis shows a highly-competitive industry that is only going to become more so. In short, they show an industry that is maturing, and thus becoming a far more difficult environment. Common changes in maturing industries include (Porter, 1980):

- Slowing growth means more competition for market share

- More selling to experienced, repeat buyers (adult and graduate students?)
- Greater emphasis on cost and service
- Increased changes in marketing, services, accounting
- New products and applications are harder to come by
- Competition increases from far away (online, international)
- Industry profits often fall, sometimes permanently

When industries change, mistakes are commonly made. Perceptions of the industry and one's own organization become less accurate. Flawed strategies that are in place or proposed are often not recognized as flawed. Organizations tend to make major investment in projects that will not yield significant returns. For example, some private universities facing declines in traditional enrollment due to changing demographics and increased competition have chosen to double-down on the traditional market, making significant investments in campus infrastructure in an attempt to draw traditional students. While this strategy might be successful when combined with other strategies, it is not likely to work on its own. "Build it and they will come" is not likely to be an effective strategy in a maturing industry.

For others, the reduced profitability of a maturing industry is problematic. Some institutions are unwilling to accept lower financial performance, and thus continue hefty tuition increases despite increasing price competition. Other recognize that things are changing, but show resentment or irrational reactions to price competition. Others blindly increase discount rates in an attempt to maintain enrollment numbers. Some institutions overemphasize new programs rather than improving and aggressively selling existing programs.

Clinging to higher quality or reputation as an excuse for not meeting aggressive pricing moves of competitors is another common mistake in maturing industries. As industries mature, quality differentials tend to erode, and private higher education is not exempt. As a result, many institutions who highly treasure their perceptions of quality and reputation will be unwilling to accept that what was formerly high quality is now medium quality, and must therefore be priced accordingly.

External analysis by itself is insufficient in terms of determining strategies. External analysis provides only the opportunities and threats side of strategic analysis; it must be combined with an analysis of internal strengths, weaknesses, and competitive advantage to be useful. Nevertheless, the external analysis in this chapter leads to several issues that should be considered in strategy formulation. Those issues include the fact that private universities, especially those with a total enrollment of fewer than 2000 students, should closely examine their competitive positions and sources of competitive advantage. They should consider that, in a mature industry, it is no longer possible to be all things to all people. Thus, they should consider adjusting and trimming degree programs and major/minor offerings to focus on programs that provide them with a competitive advantage. These include programs with distinctive advantages where competition is lower; they might also include programs where customers are low-maintenance and relatively price insensitive.

It is difficult to determine which programs provide competitive advantage without having the ability to understand the profit dynamics of each program. Few private IHEs have financial reporting systems that allow them to know the profitability of each program. Many have systems that break out direct costs of programs, at least at the department or school level, if not the program level. But few have systems that allow for an understanding of the revenue dynamics of each program and its total costs, including pertinent overhead allocations that take into account the actual costs programs.

When a university has a financial reporting system that reveals the profitability of programs, it usually finds that the vast majority of programs are not profitable. This then allows for some important questions to be asked, such as:

1. If a program is not profitable, is there a combination of revenue enhancements and cost trimming that can make the program profitable?

2. If it is unlikely that a program can be made profitable, and the program is not central to the mission of the institution, should the program be discontinued?

3. If it is unlikely that a program can be made profitable, but the program is critical to the mission of the institution, is it possible to raise the money necessary to support the program?

When the profit characteristics of a program are known, it also becomes possible to adjust pricing to reflect costs. Most private IHEs charge traditional undergraduate tuition at a flat rate that fails to take into account the demand for or costs of a program. In mature industries, it becomes more important to adjust pricing to reflect costs, which implies that programs should be charged individually, not at flat rates. At the very least, universities should consider tuition surcharges for expensive programs and those in high demand.

Given that it is typically easier to retain existing customers rather than recruit new ones, diversifying offerings to existing students is a strategy worth considering. For example, 5th-year masters degree programs offered to existing undergraduate students keep students on campus for at least an additional year. Targeting alumni for advanced degrees or credential programs may also be a profitable approach.

Maturing industries often have a "shakeout" phase, where competition drives some existing competitors out of business. This phase has begun in private higher education. In this phase, it is often possible for institutions with financial strength to acquire discounted assets from distressed competitors. The opportunity to purchase an existing campus to use as a remote location is one example; but it is also possible to pick up displaced faculty and staff members, administrators, and equipment.

Given the profitability pressures in a maturing industry, selling to the most favorable customers may be a good strategy. Offering volume discounts, such as contractual agreements with businesses, schools, or health care organizations who provide substantial numbers of students for particular degree programs, is one way to do this. In doing so, it is important to seek customers who value the differentiation that the institution already has in place, rather than those who seek excessive customization; customization is costly, and offering discounts while providing customization is normally a money-losing strategy.

Conclusion

Two strategic tools for analyzing the external environment were presented in this chapter: STEP analysis and the Five-Forces model. STEP analysis provides insights into the external environment, while the Five-Forces model provides insights into competition in the industry. Together, these tools provide an understanding of the opportunities and threats facing the organization. They also show that private higher education has entered the maturity phase. The chapter concluded by setting forth implications for private higher education; these implications demonstrate that business as usual is unlikely to be an effective strategy for most private IHEs; therefore, potential strategies were examined. These tools and the resulting analysis demonstrate how powerful and necessary external analysis is for effective strategic planning.

For additional reading

Grant Thornton (2016). The state of higher education in 2016.
Retrieved from
https://www.grantthornton.com/issues/library/whitepapers
/nfp/2016/SoHE-2016/State-of-higher-ed-2016-
overview.aspx

Porter, M. E. (2008). The competitive forces that shape
strategy. *Harvard Business Review*, 86 (1), pp.78-93.

Porter, M. E. (1980). The transition to industry maturity. *Competitive
strategy*. New York: Simon & Schuster Macmillan Co., pp.
237-253.

Weiss, M., and Selingo, J. J. (2016, October 6). 2026: The decade
ahead. *The Chronicle of Higher Education*.

4
Differentiate or Decline:

Competitive Advantage is the Key to Success

If you have read the book to this point, chances are that the strategies that have worked well for your university in the past are no longer delivering the results that you need. In case you haven't recognized it by now, the strategic landscape for higher education has irrevocably shifted. The golden age of higher education, when enrollment and access to capital were never a serious concern, is gone. In its place is a strategic world in which the majority of competitors in the marketplace have a similar value proposition. This leaves universities exposed to market forces that have caused dozens of universities to suffer declines in enrollment, reductions in force, and in some cases, closure.

There is good news, however. Universities similar to yours are enjoying significant success by using a differentiation strategy anchored in a strong competitive advantage.

Signs Your Competitive Advantage is Weak

Perhaps you are a faculty member, administrator, president, or board member. You are witnessing your university struggle to react to these new market changes and events. There's a reason you find the results of such plans underwhelming. No matter how hard a university may try, simply repeating yesterday's strategy will not bring the university the enrollment gains and financial security your university is seeking. All of the effort and capital in the world can't overcome a weak (or missing) competitive advantage.

Do any of these symptoms sound familiar?

High Tuition Discount Percentage. That percentage of the total tuition price tag that is given back to the student in the form of an enrollment incentive or "scholarship" continues to grow. Healthy universities have a discount rate under 40 percent. As the discount rate climbs above 40 percent, the net revenue position on each additional student shrinks. When the rate climbs into the 50's, it becomes a red flag. If the rate goes into the 60's, the university approaches a position where the net revenue position on additional enrollment can actually be negative.

Losing Access to Federal Monies. If the university's fiscal health deteriorates significantly, it may impact the university's financial ratios that are reported annually to the Department of Education (DOE). Several universities have been placed on heightened cash monitoring status by the DOE, which then limits the university's access to federal financial aid dollars.[13]

Accreditation Problems Related to Finances and/or Strategic Planning. Closely related to the previous point are actions taken by the university's accrediting body related to a weak financial position. In many cases, the accrediting body may also comment on

[13] https://www.insidehighered.com/quicktakes/2015/07/14/education-department-updates-cash-monitoring-list

the university's strategic plans. In both cases, action and follow up are typically required on the part of the university's leadership.

Declining Enrollment. The surest sign of a weak competitive position is a significant decline in enrollment, beyond the typical annual fluctuations. Universities in such a position may lose 10, 20, or 30 percent of their enrollments—or more—in such cases. This is a dramatic threat to annual cash flows used to fund operations.

Any combination of the above symptoms should be a red flag to you that there is some amount of weakness present in your competitive advatange and/or value proposition

The Number 1 Question You Have to Answer

A few years ago, a prospective MBA student sat in one of our offices and asked a great question: "Why should I attend your MBA program when I can drive just 10 miles down the road and attend the state university and pay much less?" According to his logic, he knew that if he graduated from their program, he'd get a good job since so many big employers recruit their graduates, and he'd pay a lot less because of the state-sponsored tuition rate.

This is an all-too-common question that you have, no doubt, heard in your career as well. A great answer doesn't require you to be the world's best salesman if your answer is backed by a powerful value proposition. Make no mistake, this is the most important question you will ever be asked, and answering it for your university is one of the most important things you can do. Your answer will determine whether you close the sale quickly or be thrust into a price war where there are no victors.

So how does your university currently answer this question? The authors have consulted with dozens of universities and have noticed the difficulty with which university administrators answer this most important strategic question:

"Why should I enroll here?"

If you or your university's administrators have difficulty answering this question, take heart—you are not alone. In their extensive book, *Creating Competitive Advantage*, authors Smith & Flanagan[14] asked 1000 corporate executives to describe their company's competitive advantage. To their surprise, only *two* out of a thousand could accurately express an answer based on competitive advantage. Most executives in this research answered ...

- Price
- Quality of product
- Good customer service

If you can't answer this question with a quick, concise answer, with facts to back it up, it should be a red flag to you that your campus has some work to do in understanding and communicating its competitive advantage.

Reasons why your current strategy isn't working

Smith & Flanagan's research went on to discuss the five fatal flaws of most companies that suffer from competitive advantage

---

[14] Smith, J. & Flanagan, W. (2006). *Creating competitive advantage.* New York: Currency Doubleday.

problems. Arguably, these five flaws are just as prevalent in non-profit higher education as they are in corporate America.

- Your campus thinks it has a competitive advantage when it really doesn't
- Your campus has a competitive advantage but doesn't know what it is—so it lowers the price instead.
- Your campus knows what its competitive advantage is, but neglects to tell prospective students about it.
- Your campus mistakes "strengths" for competitive advantage.
- Your campus doesn't concentrate on competitive advantage when making strategic and operational decisions.

The good news is that any campus can overcome these problems! Your campus can quickly and easily identify your competitive advantages, create new ones, and stay ahead of the competition.

Why price isn't a viable option for private universities

In his groundbreaking book, *Competitive Advantage*,[15] Harvard's Michael Porter describes the two basic sources of competitive advantage for any firm: price and differentiation. Having a cost advantage and competing on price means that the "cumulative internal cost of performing all value activities is lower than competitor's costs."[16] Private universities generally have a difficult time using price as a basis for competition because their direct competitors, the state university and/or community college systems, are the direct recipients of state tax dollars which allow state

---

[15] Porter, M. E. (1985). *Competitive Advantage.* NY: The Free Press.
[16] Ibid., p. 97.

universities to offer tuition rates that are much lower than private university rates—regardless of how efficiently and effectively a private university is run! While the amount appropriated for higher education varies widely from state to state, the amount is generally enough to allow state-supported universities to claim a significant amount of market share on price alone.

We spoke with Jeff Spear,[17] CEO of the firm CFO Colleague—which helps universities chart a healthy strategy from a financial perspective—about why private universities have such a difficult time playing the pricing game. Spear gave the following example: "At one university, even with a freshman discount rate higher than 60 percent, they still missed their recruitment and net tuition goals. The President believed that a bunch more students could have been recruited if they had merely moved to 64 percent. They had recruited around 200 freshmen and I was told that a mere four percent adjustment in price would have yielded another 10-to-12 freshmen. The stage was set for a conversation about net pricing. My explanation was that they were currently charging about $20,000 for tuition, so a 60 percent discount meant that they gleaned 40 percent of tuition, or $8,000 on a net basis. An increase to a 64% discount meant that they would have netted 36% of tuition, or $7,200. It just so happens that moving from collecting 40 percent down to 36 percent is a one-tenth reduction in price ($8,000 – 10% = $7,200). So, at a cursory level, one would think that a 10% increase in students recruited would be needed in order to offset the price decline. In

---

[17] Personal email conversation. June 2016.

reality, that would not be enough. Assuming 200 students at $8,000 of net tuition per student, an overall net tuition of $1,600,000 results. Taking ten percent more students (220) at the 10 percent lower price of $7,200 yields $1,584,000. It's close, but still less than what was achieved at the 60 percent discount. And, according to the President, a gain of 10 to 12 students would have been a stretch goal for his recruiting team. Indeed, the recruiting team would need to generate over 22 new students at the new discount rate just to break even (222.22 x $7,200 = $1.6 million)! The university claims victory for the incredible increase in students recruited, but has nothing additional, and often less, to show for it. All because we presume that an average of $800 in added financial aid would have brought in another 11.1 percent of student demand. That seemed far-fetched."

The bottom line? Discount rate escalation does not have a solid theoretical framework supporting its use, particularly as it approaches the stratosphere. Universities that compete on price in this manner are finding that reductions in demand make it necessary to *reduce* discounts and rely on bringing in those who are drawn to the university due to programs, reputation, or other non-price reasons.

Successful private universities typically compete using Porter's second basis for competition: differentiation. To be differentiated, according to Porter, is to build different features and services into the product line so that the consumer is willing to pay a premium price. This goes far beyond simply characterizing your programs as being "high quality." As we will show in the next chapter, differentiation arises out of a specific activity in your internal value chain. While private universities are rife with differences vis-à-vis the state universities, the key takeaway is that the difference generating our competitive advantage needs to be important *in the mind of the consumer.* Just because a private university has something that is different doesn't mean that it's also valuable to prospective students. Therefore, it is critical that private universities know and understand the buyer's value chain. Only then can we turn something different into a true competitive advantage.

Who's Buying? The Critical First Step

It's critical to any university to *correctly* identify who its customers really are. As we learned in chapter 3, any typical private university will have approximately three generic categories of customers: (a) the traditional student and his/her parents, (b) companies that hire students after graduation, and (c) adult/graduate students. Why is it so important to identify each customer base? Because to effectively differentiate a university's offerings, it's necessary to understand the effect of the university's degree programs on the personal value chain of each group of customers.

Traditional Students and Parents. Traditional-aged students, those 18-23 year olds, are the predominate customers for the traditional residential campus experience. They come to campus for a multitude of reasons, including academics, athletics, personal relationships, legacy reasons, or perhaps this was the only school mom and dad would pay for them to attend. The parents of such students are often the ones who are making the purchase, and are thus influential to the purchase decision, while the actual student is the end-user of the degree program. As deans, we have witnessed the stark differences between the value chain of the parents versus the value chain of the prospective student. Regardless of their reason, it's important to distinguish that the residential university experience will occur at a transformational time in this customer's life. This fact drives a certain mix of student services that are distinctly different from other customer groups.

Adult/Graduate Students. Adult students are so identified, usually, by their age. They might participate in the university experience through an adult degree-completion program or a graduate degree program. What makes this category of students uniquely different is their status in life. For most, life has already happened. They have life responsibilities with children, church, civic groups, employers, etc. Thus, they tend to view the university experience as a transactional experience. They know what they want, why they want it, and what they are going to do with it after graduation.

Employers. Employers are often not thought of as customers of the university, but they are in a significant way. Employers have a pulling effect on the enrollment function of the university. Employers who demand graduates with a certain set of knowledge, skills, and abilities can be well-served by universities that can shape the outcomes of the degree to match the employer's needs. By showcasing this relationship, a university can influence the prospective student's purchase decision to the extent that employment after graduation is a part of the prospective student's value chain.

Understand what your customers really want from you

Once a university understands the different types of customers it services, it must then understand two critical elements: (a) the customer's value chain, and (b) the university's value chain. Since the university's value chain will be covered in the next chapter, we will limit our discussion here to the customer's value chain. As we stated in the previous section, buyers can be categorized into groups that are roughly defined by who is making the purchase decision: traditional students/parents, employers, and adult/graduate students. While it is not possible to conclusively know the value chain decision process for every single prospective student, we can speak in generalities. According to Porter,[18] the value chain of buyers is typically driven by one of two different motives: to reduce cost, or to increase outcomes.

Reducing Cost. It's very tempting to immediately think of the individual student when considering cost and reduce the price tag of tuition at the point of sale. It's also very common to find universities that rely too heavily on "cutting a deal" with individual students because the university concludes that cutting the tuition price is the best way to land new students. Not unexpectedly, this follows on the heels of the national conversation on the affordability of a university education. If used heavily, however, a university suffers an increasing tuition discount rate and a shrinking of per-

---

[18] Porter, M.E. (1985). *Competitive Advantage*. NY: The Free Press.

student net tuition dollars used to fund operations. At a point, increasing enrollment actually *hurts* the university if the net revenue from tuition (excluding room & board) is less than the per FTE cost of operations. In reality, the best place to consider cost is when the buyer is institutional (a corporation). By demonstrating to the corporation that hiring graduates from your university actually lowers their cost in the short or long term, then you have found a perfect way to position your university's programs for competitive advantage. Thus, unless an university has an endowment resource of sufficient size to offset a state university's cost advantage, it should avoid seeking to increase enrollment by offering prospective students ever-increasing discounts.

Increasing the Buyer's Outcomes. The value chain for a prospective student buyer, whether traditional or adult/graduate, will be influenced heavily by outcomes tied to degree completion or the conclusion of the university experience. At this point, your buyer pool separates. The adult/graduate students, who we mentioned previously as being very transactional in their view of the educational experience, will have an acute focus on the career-oriented outcomes tied to the degree. They don't go back to school because they miss living in the dorms, eating cafeteria food, and going to the game on weekends. Their lives are already full. Thus, they tend to focus on the raise, promotion, or expanded career opportunities the degree brings. A university that can effectively communicate outcomes, will have a significant advantage over ones that don't.

Traditional students' buying chain contains two parts: What happens on-campus during the degree program, and what happens after graduation. If the prospective student's parents are a significant voice in the decision, be aware that two main factors tend to dominate this mechanism: affordability (not necessarily price), and employability after graduation. The on-campus value chain will be a complex mix of elements such as relationships (personal, faculty, staff), athletic opportunities, degree options, housing, proximity to entertainment, and other factors. The traditional student is often the primary decision-maker regarding these factors. Thus, a university should want to examine its differentiation in affordability, employability, and student life/services.

Okay, so what do we do now?

Take the next step by affirmatively examining your university's competitive advantage(s). If it is unclear what your competitive advantage is or whether your university has one at all, it may be helpful to have a series of brainstorming sessions with select members of faculty, staff, and alumni who have the benefit of a longitudinal view of the university. Such questions as the ones listed below are helpful in focusing this discussion:

- What are we known for?
- What category of students do we serve?
- What do our prospective students want?
- What can we do that no one else can do?
- How are we different from our competitors?
- How can we uniquely deliver our educational

products/services?

- What can we quantify, prove, and keep our competitors from easily duplicating?

Once you have gathered the broad-based information from the brainstorming sessions, you're ready to move on to the next chapter and examine your internal value chain in greater detail.

5
IDENTIFYING YOUR COMPETITIVE ADVANTAGE

What's the best way to identify a university's competitive advantage? As academic administrators, it's a part of the job to be able to answer this question. As administrators, we know that it is a hard truth that some areas of the academic enterprise are cash generators, while others are cash users. It's tempting to answer the opening question by quoting the many statistics a university already gathers for external reporting purposes. Metrics such as gross tuition revenue, student credit hours sold, enrollment headcount, and FTE are commonly used as a measure of success that presidents, board members, donors, external reporting agencies, and creditors need to hear.

There's a problem, however, with using these trackable metrics to analyze the competitive position for universities. These metrics are all reactionary. They do an excellent job of telling us what has already occurred, but they don't do a very good job of explaining *why* those cash generating programs on your campus are doing well, or conversely, why a program that once enrolled great numbers is now performing poorly.

For tuition-driven universities, the truth of the matter is that it's all about net tuition cash flows. If you want to increase your cash flow, you have to increase enrollment. If you want to increase enrollment, you have to convince prospective students that your programs are more valuable than those of your competitors. If you want to increase both the real and perceived value of your programs, you have to analyze the program's competitive advantage.

It's just that simple.

What is a competitive advantage?

Simply defined, a competitive advantage is built on the foundation of an organizational resource or activity that, when measured against our direct competitors, the firm does better than anyone else. Thus, having a competitive advantage over the competition provides an irrefutable advantage when seeking new customers. This is the preferred strategy for private universities, as it plays to their natural advantages. However, as we learned earlier from the research of Smith & Flanagan, not all corporate executives can accurately define their competitive advantage. We have found this to be true within higher education as well.

Try this simple exercise. Ask yourself (or better yet, ask your admissions office), what sells my university? Why would anyone want to enroll here as opposed to the university down the street? What's the compelling reason for any student to enroll? If your answer to any of the above questions includes responses such as the ones listed below, you know you have some work to do in defining where your competitive advantage lies:

- We have a pretty campus
- We have a loving campus community and small class sizes
- We teach quality classes/programs
- Here you're not just a number, you're a name
- We have great student service

There's nothing inherently wrong with any of these statements except that this is the *exact same value proposition* as almost every other small private university in the United States. Therefore, continuing to sell your degree programs using this language only further drives you toward price competition by giving the student the impression that all colleges are exactly the same and that their distinctives are meaningless. In the next chapter, you will learn that once you identify your competitive advantage, the language you use to sell your value proposition needs to change as well. For now, it's enough for us to know that an effective competitive advantage needs to conform to the following:[19]

- A competitive advantage is quantifiable
- A competitive advantage can be proved
- A competitive advantage cannot be easily duplicated
- A competitive advantage is (usually) sustainable

---

[19] Riggs, B. (2014). Achieving Sales Excellence. Tulsa, OK: Gladius Enterprises Publications.

Based on our research, here are a few examples of universities with an apparent competitive advantage:

- Newman University (KS) has the largest high-school dual enrollment population of any private college in the state of Kansas (distribution channel)

- Oklahoma Wesleyan University (OK) embraces its conservative theological heritage by integrating its Christian faith into all courses and degrees (product attributes)

- Point Loma Nazarene University (CA) and Palm Beach Atlantic University (FL) exploit their respective geographic proximity to the beach for their advantage (best location)

- The King's College (NYC) exploits its proximity to the New York City business market for student internships and job placement (employer relationships)

- LeTourneau University's (TX) unique history and deep competencies and facilities in aviation and engineering allow it to recruit a significantly higher percentage of STEM students. (unique teaching/learning)

- Indiana Wesleyan University (IN) obtained a first-mover advantage by opening dozens of satellite campus locations to facilitate the teaching of adult/graduate degree programs. (market timing/first-mover advantage)

- Liberty University (TN) gained significant market share by investing heavily into their online platform supporting 100 percent online degree programs (responsiveness to a changing market)

- Adrian College (MI) gained significant enrollment by adding athletic programs and academic programs that were unique and not duplicated by either state or private university competitors. (product attributes)

- Grace College (IN) scrapped its traditional 4 year degree model and made every undergraduate degree on campus achievable in 3 years. (product attributes)

- Southern Nazarene University (OK) embraced its feeder network of denominational churches such that the university has the highest population of traditional students from those churches of any Nazarene university. (distribution channel)

- Azusa Pacific University (CA) leverages its strength in music and theatre with its proximity to Hollywood to provide students with excellent internships and jobs in the entertainment industry (employer relations)

Core Activity or Competitive Advantage?

In order to determine the strength of a competitive advantage, you first have to identify it. There's a critical distinction between a university's core activities (competencies) and a competitive advantage that is useful in this discussion. Let's use a simple example to illustrate this. In the world of discount retailing, the major competitors are Walmart, Kmart, Sears, and Target. When you step back and look at the basic business activities of these companies, what do you see? Given some minor differences, they all do the exact same thing: retail merchandising, logistics, and basic customer services. It's not until you ask yourself the next question that the power of competitive advantage becomes apparent. Out of all these competitors performing basically the same activities as everyone else, *who is the best at each activity?* Walmart creams the competition in both retail merchandising and logistics. It's not even close. But it didn't happen overnight. Walmart built this advantage incrementally over two decades. It began with location (small towns) where Walmart didn't have significant competition and could charge slightly higher prices than the chain did elsewhere. From there, the corporation was an early adopter of backwards integration into its distribution channel by building its own network of distribution centers and buying its own fleet of trucks. The internal cost savings provided by these and many other initiatives allowed Walmart to pass the savings on to the customer, which gives Walmart a significant price advantage over its competitors. So powerful is Walmart's competitive advantage, that Target chose to stock higher quality products to avoid direct competition, while Kmart has flirted with bankruptcy for the past two decades. A final tidbit of knowledge: Walmart was able to drive itself to this level of success and market dominance in an era when profit margins were impossibly thin (2-3 percent) and smaller competitors were permanently closing (e.g., Woolco, King's, Korvette's, etc.). Doesn't that environment sound familiar to what's happening right now in higher education? That's the power of a well-researched and well-executed competitive advantage.

Let's move our example back into private higher education. Think about your university and its three largest competitors. When you step back, you'll see that all of the universities have essentially the same core activities: teaching students (instruction), student services, student life (including athletics), and external relations (alumni services, career services, and advancement). [20] Now for every activity, ask yourself, "Who's the best?" Until you identify for your university where you have a competitive advantage over the competition, you won't know where to strategically align your institutional resources and drive enrollment gains. As you begin to analyze your value chain in detail, you will no doubt see elements where you possess a competitive advantage (ours is better than theirs), a competitive disadvantage (theirs is better than ours), or competitive parity (ours is equal to theirs).

Examining Your University's Core Activities

Let's continue by understanding the university's value chain.

Unlike a company that manufacturers a tangible product, a university education and its delivery is not only a service, but it is also intangible. As you can see from the figure, a university's resources and capabilities form the foundation of its core

---

[20] The authors realize that this list of activities oversimplifies the value chain of the university. The generic descriptors of core activities provided here are for purposes of illustration.

activities. One or more of these core activities may become a competitive advantage. A competitive advantage that is stable over time or is replicable over time can be classified as a sustainable competitive advantage. Thus, we have to look closely at the core activities that add incremental value to the degree experience that can form the foundation of a differential competitive advantage. In his classic work, *Competitive Advantage*, Michael Porter[21] provides a list of the representative sources of differentiation within a value chain that can be adapted to this discussion.

1. Sourcing
   a. Superior training of faculty and staff members
   b. The development of proprietary technology that aids either the student experience, faculty advising, or the delivery of student services.
   c. Academic and/or benefit programs to attract the best faculty members
2. Daily Operations
   a. Programs to retain the best faculty members
   b. Degree and Certificate programs with unique features
   c. Rapid introduction of new degree programs
   d. Unique teaching/learning experiences or delivery methods
   e. High quality students
   f. Attractive campus facilities (as a signal to academic quality, not beauty alone)
   g. Responsiveness to changes in the market
   h. Unique term schedules
   i. Best campus location(s)
   j. Ability to service students anywhere
   k. Single point of contact solutions for paying tuition,

---

[21] Porter, M.E. (1985). *Competitive Advantage*. NY: The Free Press.

academic advisement, and other student services.

3. Marketing & Sales
   a. Recruiting better qualified sales & service personnel
   b. Superior media research
   c. Speed of information delivery to prospective students regarding admissions, financing, and degree completion schedules.
   d. Most desirable media placements
   e. Product positioning and image (reputation)
   f. High advertising level and quality
   g. Personal relationships with community colleges, high schools, and other supply channels
   h. Personal relationships with institutional "buyers" (corporate affiliate relationships)
   i. Superior technical literature, website information, & other sales aids
   j. Most extensive promotion
4. Alumni (Service after the Sale)
   a. Extensive training of alumni personnel
   b. Depth and quality of services offered to alumni
   c. Additional training and educational opportunities provided

While this list is not exhaustive, it does represent a good cross-section of the core activities of a private university. Any one of the above activities has the potential to become a competitive advantage for an university given the right investment of time and resources. Since every university's competitive position is unique, we encourage you to study the above list and compare it to the activities at your university. From there, make a list (strategically) as to which elements of your university's core activities are the most well developed, thus providing the best starting point to give your university a competitive edge against the competition.

The VRIO Framework

Jay Barney, in his masterwork, *Creating and Sustaining Competitive Advantage*,[22] introduces a valuable resource for firms to analyze the state of their core activities. We are going to adapt it for our use in private higher education. The VRIO framework allows the firm to view its activities through the lens of its resources to determine whether or not its activities form the basis of a competitive advantage. As with the core activity list outlined above, these core activities may be any form of university strength or particular competency. VRIO is simply an acronym for the four simple questions firms ask when using the model: Is it **Valuable**? Is it **Rare**? Is it costly or difficult to **Imitate**? Is our firm **Organized** to use this resource or competency to our advantage? We can use this simple framework to make great discoveries within the university. We simply apply this framework to each of the core activities we defined for ourselves above. Let's take a closer look at each question and how they it be answered for your university.

Is It Valuable? The question of value must be considered through the eyes of our prospective students and/or the companies that hire them. For a university strength to have value, it must be valuable to situations or customers external to the organization. Does it create value in the mind of the prospective students? Since academic degree programs provide qualifications for professional careers post-graduation, it is appropriate to review the outcomes of your university's degree portfolio. Can graduates of your degree

---

[22] Barney, J. (2011) *Creating and Sustaining a Competitive Advantage*, 4th ed. Upper Saddle River, NJ: Prentice Hall

programs sit for professional licensure examinations? Enter graduate school at other universities? Most degree programs at accredited universities will be able to answer "yes" to the question of value.

Is It Rare? The question of rarity is particularly important. Are we the only university that provides this academic program, service, co-curricular activity, or athletic opportunity? Many universities offer high-quality academic programs and services, but unfortunately, they aren't rare among the competition. It is always easier to compete if you offer the only option in town! For example, in 2015, Sullivan University offered a degree in Nannying, while the Minneapolis College of Art & Design offered a degree in Comic Art.

To be rare, it is not necessary to be unique. It is necessary, however, to have some competency that is not widely shared or common. For example, you might be the only university of your type or in your region with a particular program. Other universities may have the same program, but those other universities are so geographically separated that your university is unique within its geographical region. Or they have such a different mission that they are not your competitors.

Is It Costly or Difficult to Imitate? It stands to reason that an university would not want to see its uniqueness easily duplicated by competing campuses. Yet, many a competitive advantage has been undermined by competitor's replication. Therefore, it is critical to ask, "Can this strength be easily imitated or replicated by the competition?" The extent to which replication is difficult will determine the time period of any advantage. For example, universities began offering adult-oriented, lockstep, modular, and time-compressed degree completion programs heavily in the 1990's. A hallmark of these programs was the accelerated class format. Instead of a traditional 16-week class format, these programs offered classes in 5-8 week formats. When introduced, these programs were difficult to duplicate as it required a competitor to change curriculum, academic term structures, and financial aid packaging policies to match. These changes were often difficult to implement at competing universities, thus providing a significant barrier to entry into the market. Today, however, nearly all universities have replicated these features and offset any competitive benefit they once provided.

Organized to Benefit? – Regardless of the portfolio of institutional strengths and core activities, a university must have an organizational structure capable of deploying these strengths for the purposes of differentiating the university from the competition and therefore driving enrollment. Let's hypothesize an example. Assume that XYZ University has permission to offer a specialized Master of Science degree with a major in the Cure for Cancer. This is obviously very popular as it is the only one in the country. Student enrollment isn't an issue and neither is student employment after graduation. Lab space can be easily built with the grant funding that is readily available. However, because of its unique subject area, it is impossible for XYZ to find the professors to teach it. Thus, the program isn't offered, the labs are never built, and the students never enroll. This is the essence of having an organization that is organized to exploit its advantages. In this case, XYZ cannot deploy this program because it lacks a certain part of the organizational competency.

Let's look at a real example from the tire industry

By all accounts, Stanley Gault had a fabulous career behind him. As the CEO of Rubbermaid throughout the 1980's, he had driven the company's sales to a five-fold increase by focusing his efforts on lean operations coupled with heavy investment in research & development. At one point, Rubbermaid produced more than 100 new products per year. His efforts transformed a declining business into one of America's most admired corporations. After his retirement from Rubbermaid in the spring of 1991, he was offered the CEO position at Goodyear just three weeks later. Gault had twice before turned down this position, stating that he was happy to simply serve on the board. However, this time he accepted and immediately began to impress his vision of leadership upon his new company. Goodyear was experiencing a multi-year slide in profitability, to which Gault applied his tried-and-true formulas. He attacked the debt, sold off non-core assets, raised capital, and invested heavily in new product lines.

Gault became famous for visiting showrooms and factory floors during off hours and on weekends to discover the inside story of operations or to test the market for new ideas. On one trip to a factory, he discovered a new tire design (that would become the Aquatred). In quizzing the researchers who developed the tire, Gault discovered that this tire could do something that no other tire could do at the time—channel water away from the underside of the tire and increase traction on the road. Unfortunately, the tire had been in development for years with no end in sight. Even with such a revolutionary breakthrough, the tire wasn't even on the market! This was a well-known and notorious problem in the tire market. Research and development of new tire designs often took years and companies trickled out new designs at a slow pace to the market. Gault wasted no time in launching this and other products into the lucrative replacement tire market as opposed to the dealer tire market, where profit margins were smaller.

The result of Gault's efforts was astounding. The company sold over 1 million tires in its first year of production, 20 percent more than was forecast. The factory producing the tires quickly moved to three shifts and had to increase its workforce by 13 percent just to handle the increased demand. "Gault set an impressive record in his 4-$1/2$ years at Goodyear. The compound annual growth rate of earnings-per-share before extraordinary items and accounting changes from 1991 through 1994 was 82.2 percent. The compound annual average income growth from continuing operations before extraordinary items during the same period was 96.7 percent. Gault set up new distribution channels that expanded the company's reach through outlets such as WalMart, Sears, Kmart, Montgomery Ward, and Penske AutoCenters."[23] By every measure, Gault succeeded.

Let's look at the Aquatred tire through the lens of the VRIO framework. The first question, "Is it valuable?" is easy to answer. Is

---

[23] Donlon, J.P. (December 1, 1995). A New Spin for Goodyear. *Chief Executive*. Retrieved June 22, 2016.

it valuable for the customer to be able to have increased traction in wet conditions so as to avoid accidents and slippery conditions? Of course the answer is yes. But several competitors might also claim that their tire had good traction. So this answer alone isn't enough to establish a competitive advantage. The second question, "Is it rare?" is likewise easy to answer—yes. The researchers were convinced that the design of their tire exceeded anything else on the market. However, rarity as a stand-alone variable doesn't make for a winning formula. In fact, the uniqueness of the tire's design led many executives to question whether its odd tread appearance would negatively affect sales. The third question, "Is it costly or difficult to imitate?" would also give us the answer we are looking for—yes. Whether the slow pace of R&D in the industry was due to the complexity of the tire design or due to an organizational culture of slowness, the effect is the same. Gault knew it would take competitors years to match the design of the Aquatred with one of their own. The final question, "Are we organized to benefit this?" was a resounding "no." Gault knew he had discovered a winning tire formula that day, but because the tire wasn't in production or on the market, it wasn't bringing in new revenue. The organization wasn't currently benefitting from it. Therefore, it wasn't helping Goodyear. Thus, Goodyear had only to deploy the Aquatred to change the result of the organization question from "no" to "yes," which it did less than a year later.

Was the tire design *valuable* to Goodyear?	Yes
Was the tire design *rare*?	Yes
Was the tire design costly or difficult to *imitate*?	Yes
Was Goodyear *organized* to exploit this tire design?	No

The example of the Aquatred tire at Goodyear provides several valuable lessons that we can transfer to the higher education industry and our use of the VRIO framework.

Lesson #1: VRIO is a snapshot

The VRIO framework is a simple tool, but it is to be used with caution. Like most tools or formulas, the end result changes if you change the inputs. What kept the Aquatred from having four affirmative responses, thus being labeled as a source of competitive advantage? The answer was the fact that the organization wasn't exploiting the opportunity. We know the end of the story; the Aquatred became a huge success when it was released. Had we evaluated the tire one year later, the result would have changed. Be mindful in your use of the VRIO framework that time and circumstances can change the outcome of your analysis.

Lesson #2: Leadership is key

What kept the tire from the market? It was a lengthy process to bring a new tire to market. Gault knew he had to make a change in that process if he was to bring the tire out quickly. In most organizations, it takes both the right level of authority and the right leadership personality to make change happen. Gault had both. He was the CEO, which gave him the authority to make changes as he wished. But he also had a well-honed leadership style which helped him gain his followers' trust—a necessary precursor to a change effort. As you use the VRIO framework, you'll undoubtedly uncover several strengths, resources, and capabilities in your university's core activities that may only be one answer away from being classified as a source of competitive advantage. In many cases, it will take effective leadership to move these into the four star category.

Lesson #3: VRIO is Followed by Planning

VRIO by itself isn't a plan because it isn't designed to be. Stanley Gault had to effectively plan for this new product's introduction. He devised a plan that included such elements as releasing multiple tires at the same time to offset any possible negative effects stemming from the Aquatred's odd appearance, raising significant working capital through additional stock sales to fund the product launch, and rushing development of companion products to capitalize on the interest of the customer in the main product. Each of these steps took, time, coordinated effort, and corporate focus. A well-coordinated strategic plan is key to maximizing a competitive advantage.

Build on Your Identified Advantages

In using the VRIO framework, you will undoubtedly identify your university's competitive advantage. If you find that your university already has a known competitive advantage, the next step may be to build upon that advantage. Anderson University (IN) is a comprehensive university affiliated with the Church of God denomination. Anderson already counted its business school as a source of competitive advantage. The business school had significant enrollments and continued to add co-curricular programs to add value to the students' experience. However, in 1999, the faculty noticed a significant niche in the market that was underserved—other small, private, faith-based universities that needed doctorally-qualified business professors. Thus, Anderson developed a doctor of business administration (DBA) degree for the specific purpose of developing graduates who would take careers in faith-based universities with a teaching-orientation. To this end, Anderson developed its program upon three legs: teaching, research, and faith-learning integration. According to Dr. Terry Truitt, Anderson's Dean of Business, "we want to build exceptional scholar/practitioners. Teaching is important because the universities where we place our graduates are often teaching-oriented as opposed to research-oriented. Research is important because it is the nature of the business we are in. Faith-learning integration is important because the universities where our graduates are employed often have this as a part of their institutional mission. So we are able to help another institution meets its missional goals when their faculty come to us as students." [24] Upon its inception, Anderson's DBA program was unique among the degree offerings at small faith-based universities.

What If My Campus Doesn't Have a Competitive Advantage?

Dr. Robert Myers is the President of Toccoa Falls College (TFC), a faith-based school affiliated with the Christian & Missionary Alliance denomination in Georgia. Dr. Myers took the helm of TFC in 2012. The college he inherited was in a less-than-stellar competitive condition, enrollments were down, and fiscal health was weak. Said Dr. Myers, "We worked for two years to restructure our operations and balance our budget." [25]

A former business dean himself, Dr. Myers was no stranger to effective strategic planning. But TFC offered a unique challenge. The college itself was geographically remote, both the alumni and donor base were small, and total FTE enrollment was fewer than 800 students. By all accounts, the college didn't have a specific competitive advantage. As most college presidents do, he hit the road to speak to donors, churches, and other friends of the college. That's when he stumbled upon what would become one of the college's current competitive advantages: homeschool students and students in private Christian high schools who take concurrent college classes during high school. "The notion of reaching out to high school students through concurrent enrollment programs isn't new. But in our state, there aren't many universities that intentionally

---

[24] Truitt, T. Personal communication. June, 2016.
[25] Myers, R. Personal communication. June, 2016.

reach out to the homeschool community or to students in private Christian high schools. Yet our institutional mission is a great fit with that population. So we set about to make TFC concurrent-enrollment friendly. We developed programs and policies that allow local students to enroll in our campus-based classes at a discounted rate. Further, we can credential the private high school's own faculty members as being TFC faculty so that the student earns college credit while taking high school courses. We even offer support to those high school faculty members with syllabus development and course design."

The results have been significant. Myers reported that when he arrived as President, TFC only enrolled three concurrent students. Today, TFC enrolls more than 400! Prior to 2012, only one university in the state provided outreach to this part of the market. Today, TFC's reputation has driven it into the number one position and ahead of all competitors.

A second area of competitive advantage for TFC arose out of its ministry major. Like many evangelical Christian universities, TFC grants degrees in theology and ministry. Many similar universities simply have such degrees that allow a student to become ordained in a particular denomination, or serve a traditional function, such as youth ministry, music ministry, or elder care, within an American church congregation. TFC took a pragmatic approach in the development of a new major in Sustainable Community Development. Myers recounts, "We saw a need in our current student base for a ministry solution that capitalizes on the students' youthful passion for service to others. The program helps students address global problems and simultaneously fulfill God's desire to take His good news to all nations. Additionally, whether the students serve overseas or not, they are still equipped to be strategic partners in sustainability issues within their local community here at home." A donor heard of this project and funded it with a modest gift. The college used the funds to drive even more uniqueness into the program. Rather than simply make it a theoretical classroom learning experience, the college built a live learning lab in sustainable development right on campus. Since the college is blessed with acreage due to its rural location, finding space was easy. Now, students have a unique learning environment where they can put their skills in sustainable agriculture, irrigation, and livestock to work. Additionally, the donor gift made possible a visiting professorship for the new program. The program has become a unique selling point that, for the moment, isn't replicated by any of TFC's competing universities.

From this, we can take away a final lesson important in our understanding of the VRIO framework.

Lesson #4: Building a competitive advantage can take time.

If you have to build out a competitive advantage where one does not currently exist, results may take time and/or investment of resources.

For Further Reading

Barney, J. (2011) *Creating and sustaining a competitive advantage*, 4th ed. Upper Saddle River, NJ: Prentice Hall

Cummings, S., & Angwin, D. (2015). *Strategy builder: How to create and communicate more effective strategies.* UK: John Wiley & Sons.

Das, R. (2016). United Bank of India: A strategic analysis using the VRIO method. *The IUP Journal of Bank Management*, XV(2), pp. 21-37.

Tompson, G. (2015). *How strategy works: Using the strategy process cycle to develop competitive advantage.* FL: CitriClean of Florida, LLC.

6

COMMUNICATE OR DIE:
WHAT'S YOUR VALUE PROPOSITION?

As you learned in the previous chapters, your competitive advantages are why your university is in business. You should focus both on tangible and intangible competitive advantages. The best enrollment professionals today focus on the intangible sources of relative superiority, providing additional value, and a burning desire to compete strategically alongside the tangible.

Ideally, the identification of competitive advantages lead to the development of a value proposition. This is a specific claim that only your university can make and that sets you apart. The value proposition can be used to create powerful tools such as your initial introductory statement, persuasive emails, persuasive letters, and other seeding tools used in your prospective enrollment efforts. These tools achieve much of the upfront hard work for you. When you finally sit down with your prospective student, the value proposition has laid the groundwork to start the sales call off at a higher functioning level. [26]

In reality, however, many universities (and their respective recruiters) are rarely able to articulate what makes them unique. As we learned in Chapter 4, the very simple question, "Why should I enroll here?" almost always elicits a host of generic and rather trivial answers. These answers do little to rid prospects of the notion that most universities are pretty much alike and offer nearly identical degrees and programs.

As we covered earlier in the book, the typical answers to the hypothetical question, "Why should I enroll here?" are all so familiar:

- Because we offer a supportive campus community

- Because we offer quality degrees

- Because we are faith-based

- Because we have great service

- Because we offer a liberal arts education

Or because we have been here for 100+ years, or we have the prettiest campus…

The first and most obvious problem with these answers is that each of your competitors is saying exactly the same thing. It seems that every university claims to be the best and the brightest, to be the market leader, to offer the industry's highest quality, to encompass excellence, and on and on. Let's face it, have you ever heard of a university competing by stating: "We have low quality

---

[26] We recognize that the use of the term "sales" within the domain of enrollment management may cause some to react negatively. However, it is our assertion that this is the most instructional way to present the material at hand.

programs and terrible service?" Of course not! Most universities make similar claims. For prospective students, this ambiguity makes the decision process quite difficult. Without a clearly differentiated solution, how can a prospective student know which university offering is best? Think about it. Can you really make a bad choice if each product is really that good?

So, what criteria should be used to make a determination? If perceived quality is similar, then the default criterion, in the minds of students and parents, is price—and competing on price is never a good strategy for maximizing value. Universities compete on price for two significant reasons. First, they have not learned how to effectively differentiate their offerings and present a true value proposition. Second, they have convinced themselves that their industry is commoditized and price is the only thing that really matters to their customers. In this case, prospective students have done a far better job selling the universities than the universities have done in selling the students. These two factors almost guarantee that universities will continue to give away gross margin dollars and fail to maximize their revenues.

The second and less obvious problem with the answers given to the question "Why should I enroll here?" is that the language used in the reply is so vague and ambiguous that it doesn't communicate any real value in the first place. When a university claims to have "great quality," what does it really mean? A prospective student might interpret the word "quality" to mean any of the following things:

- teaching excellence of the faculty
- up-to-date campus facilities
- availability of a specific major/program
- flexibility in delivery format
- speed to graduation
- starting salary upon graduation
- alumni connections
- and much more

The same is true for service. What is great customer service in higher education? Again, for any given customer it can mean something completely different. In reality, the phrase *great service* serves no purpose whatsoever in the mind of the prospective student.

These challenges are compounded by the fact that most university recruiters have the same issues when presenting their degrees or programs. The typical recruiter is little more than a product pusher, expounding on the many can't-miss, must-have features of the degree, which leads a prospective student even further into the idea that the solution is little more than a commodity item that can be acquired from one of several good universities. The more generic and undefined your competitive advantage—and thus your value proposition—the more revenue-killing the effect will be.

Let's take a moment and provide a critical distinction. A value proposition backed by a strong competitive advantage is *distinctly different* from a savvy marketing strategy. A huge mistake that many universities make is to believe that "marketing" is akin to an ATM for the university. This line of thinking leads many institutions to invest heavily in marketing only to see their ROI on those dollars diminish rapidly. Effective marketing strategies are wonderful tools, but without an effective value proposition, the return is tepid at best. Today's prospective student wants to engage with a university via social media and other internet-driven media. In response, many private universities have become skilled in using all aspects of social media to communicate with prospective students. But what will the university showcase if it cannot communicate a compelling reason for the student to attend once that connection is made? A university's marketing strategy is a tactic used to communicate its value proposition.

The differentiation that prospective students crave will address their expressed and unexpressed needs. As more and more universities battle for fewer and fewer traditional-aged students, most will compete the only way they know how—by offering a lower price in the form of higher discount rates. However, by differentiating your university, matching the proposed solution to the student's needs, and addressing the student's critical wants and needs, a university has a far better chance of maximizing its revenues.

Okay, so what do we do now?

The first step is always to do your homework on the competition. We assume that every university has a working knowledge of its immediate competitors such that documenting a competing university's strengths and weaknesses is possible. Review the list of your competitor's strengths and weaknesses and compare with the value chain activity elements from Chapter 5, then try to answer the following questions:

- What are they known for?
- What can they do that no one else can do?
- How are they different from us?
- What do they have that is difficult for us to duplicate?
- Do they have a strength that can be easily elevated to a competitive advantage?
- Do they have a strong value proposition they are using against us?

The second step is to review the competitive analysis map below and determine the intersection between your university's competitive strengths and weaknesses in respect to the strengths and weaknesses of your primary competitors.

Competitive Analysis Map

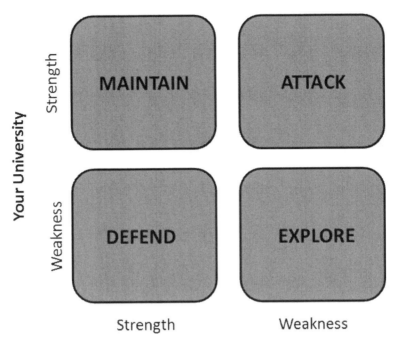

The Competition

The competitive analysis map provides for the possibility of four generic competitive situations. At the intersection of strength versus strength, we suggest using *Maintenance* tactics. In this situation, your value proposition is well developed and provides a comparable amount of market share against the competition who also shares this area of strength. At the intersection of your university's strength and the competition's weakness, we suggest using *Attack* tactics. In this situation, your value proposition is well developed and provides significant market share against the competition's weakness. At the intersection of your university's weakness and the competition's strength, we suggest *Defensive* tactics. In this situation, your university may or may not have a value proposition and your university may struggle to hold its existing market share against the competition's strength. At the intersection of shared weakness, we suggest *Exploring* a new value proposition. In both Explore and Defend, there is the distinct possibility that your university may have a weak and ineffective value proposition, or no value proposition at all. In such circumstances, it is critical that you walk through a value proposition development exercise such as the one below.

Develop A Unique Value Proposition

The third step is to develop your own value proposition. A value proposition is a statement which projects the competitive advantage (value) a prospective student could realize through the implementation of a specific unique capability or solution. That might sound complicated, but it really isn't. The value proposition stimulates interest with the prospective student and clearly differentiates your university's offerings. The value proposition—especially if supported by a reference story—is a powerful initial statement and serves as the catalyst to start a sales process cycle.

Use your value proposition in phone calls, emails, voicemails, social media postings, and presentations to help prospective students understand why it's worth their time to meet with you.

Sample Value Proposition Statements

To kick-start the process of writing value propositions for your university, here are a few samples.

Sample 1: (Employer outcomes) "ABC University's graduates from its supply chain management program saved their employers an average of $1.2 million last year. No other university helps manufacturers like ABC U does."

Sample 2: (Specialized Program & Placement) "The graduates of XYZ University's Cyber Defense Technology program become trusted leaders at some of the largest companies in the world. 100% of last year's graduating class had signed full-time job commitments *before* graduation and had the highest average starting salary of all graduates of XYZ."

Sample 3: (Speed to Completion) "Big Church University's proprietary student success coaching portal means that every student has 24/7 access to not only their classes, but also coaches, tutors, and study materials. This helps our graduates earn their degrees 20 percent faster than anyone else in the state."

Draft Your University's Value Proposition

Use the spaces below to draft a value proposition statement for your university.

_____

_____

_____

_____

_____

Value Proposition Basics to Remember

State your core promise to the prospective student in the positive:

- The problem *"XYZ University will solve this [one specific problem] for you"*
- The time frame *"XYZ will do it within this [specific time frame.]"*
- The Or-Else *"Otherwise XYZ will refund your tuition."*

State an additional promise to the prospective student in the negative:

- *This won't require any ____ from you.*
- *This won't cost you anything beyond _____.*

Restate the "Nobody else does this:"

- *Nobody else solves this one problem like XYZ does.*
- *Nobody else does it in the time frame XYZ does.*
- *Nobody else guarantees it like XYZ does.*
- *Everybody else requires ____ from you. XYZ doesn't.*
- *Everybody else also charges you for ___. XYZ doesn't.*

Having Multiple Value Propositions. Note that in the sample value proposition statements above, some were university-wide, and others were program-specific. Given that your value propositions derive from your competitive advantages, it is possible, and indeed beneficial, to have multiple value propositions. These can be used in marketing multiple programs, since students increasingly shop for specific programs.

At the same time, when you look at your sources of competitive advantage and the resulting value propositions, attempt to discern if there are patterns that form a gestalt. If so, you may discover an overarching value proposition that can be used to differentiate your university. If this overarching value proposition can be expressed as a compelling tag line, you may have developed a powerful marketing message.

Conclusion

The focus of the book to this point has been in understanding the competitive environment, developing sources of competitive advantage, and communicating your value propositions. In the next two chapters, you will learn how to state key result areas, goals, and objectives, and develop strategies and action plans.

For further reading

Girard, J., & Shook, R. (1989). *How to close every sale.* NY: Grand Central Publishing.

Lafley, A., & Martin, R. (2013). *Playing to win: How strategy really works.* Boston: Harvard Business School Publishing.

Riggs, G. B. (2013). *I didn't sign up to be in marketing.* Tulsa, OK: Perform One Institute, Inc.

7

DEVELOPING A STRATEGIC PLAN:
KEY RESULT AREAS, GOALS, AND OBJECTIVES

Writing a good strategic plan that is built upon the strong foundation of a sustainable competitive advantage and value proposition is only part of the recipe in driving enrollment at a private university. Many a good strategic plan has been derailed by the weaknesses of the plan's design and/or implementation of the plan. While the main purpose of this book remains centered on competitive advantage, we would be remiss if we did not provide a roadmap for the process of creating and implementing a strategic plan that is focused on developing and sustaining a competitive advantage for your institution. In this chapter, we will discuss how to create key result areas, goals, and objectives. In the next chapter, we will focus on the development of strategies and action plans. The process moves from big picture, general ideas about the future to specific steps necessary to bring a desired future into reality.

Mission and Vision

A mission statement is an enduring description of the purpose of your institution. Mission statements are meant to be relatively long-lasting; the purpose of your institution should not change frequently. Almost every institution of private higher education has a mission statement; many even have a good one. Having a mission statement that has been well thought out and is well written is extremely important, and the process required to do so can be difficult and lengthy. At this point, we assume that your institution has been through that process and has a good mission statement. It is important that everything in the strategic plan follow from and be consistent with the mission statement.

A mission statement does not need to be long, but it does need to describe what the purpose of the institution is. For example, the mission of Chapman University, a private institution in Southern California, is "to provide personalized education of distinction that leads to inquiring, ethical, and productive lives as global citizens."[27] Indiana Wesleyan University, a faith-based institution, states its mission as "Indiana Wesleyan University is a Christ-centered academic community committed to changing the world by developing students in character, scholarship, and leadership."[28]

In contrast to a mission statement, a vision statement describes what the institution hopes to become in the relatively near future (5-10 years). The vision statement often describes how the institution wants to be viewed in the marketplace, or how it hopes to

[27] https://www.chapman.edu/catalog/oc/current/ug/content/ 1403.htm
[28] https://www.indwes.edu/about/mission-and-commitments

have an impact within its sphere of activity. For example, Chapman's vision statement is, "Chapman University will be a preeminent university engaged in distinguished liberal arts and professional programs that are interconnected, reach beyond the boundaries of the classroom and work toward developing the whole person: the intellectual, physical, social and spiritual dimensions of life."[29] Indiana Wesleyan states its vision as, "Indiana Wesleyan University is a truly great Christian university serving the world."[30] Note that each of these vision statements communicates something about how the institution hopes to be viewed. Chapman wants to be known as a preeminent university with distinguished programs; Indiana Wesleyan wants to be known as a truly great Christian university.

Mission and vision statements are important in the quest for competitive advantage, because they can paint a picture of the quality and the uniqueness of an institution. Unfortunately, many mission and vision statements for private higher education institutions sound eerily similar, as if the same faculty committee wrote all of them. As you work toward defining, building, and sustaining competitive advantages for your institution, revision of the mission statement may be necessary, and revision of the vision will be likely, so that it reflects what your institution is becoming.

Key Result Areas

---

[29] https://www.chapman.edu/catalog/oc/current/ug/content/1403.htm
[30] https://www.indwes.edu/about/mission-and-commitments

Your institution's strategic plan will typically address a number of key result areas. These will vary from institution to institution, but typically include enrollment, operations, academic programs, finances, and advancement. For example, Indiana Wesleyan University's strategic plan is organized around the categories of great students, great people, great programs, and great scope, with goals and strategies for each area.[31] The strategic plan for the Argyros School of Business at Chapman University is organized around three areas affecting its value proposition: program excellence, industry partnerships, and brand prominence.[32] While it is not absolutely necessary to designate key result areas, it can help make the strategic plan more useful, in that it provides a small number of items for people to focus on, and helps organize the plan. It often becomes the starting point for the development of dashboards that track progress on strategic objectives.

Terminology: Goals versus Objectives

No consensus exists concerning the difference between goals and objectives, and the terms are often used interchangeably. For the purposes of strategic planning, however, it is important to differentiate between goals and objectives. In this book, therefore, we will use the following definitions:

Goals are general statements of intent that identify outcomes important to the organization. Conceptual areas of importance to the organization should be evident in the goals. Goals are the conceptual

---

[31] https://www.indwes.edu/about/administration/strategic-plan
[32] http://www.chapman.edu/business/about/strategic-plan.aspx

links that bridge the broadly stated mission and specific measurable objectives.

Objectives are specific and desired outcomes or performance targets, stated in measurable language. Objectives are the items that are directly measured. They should be linked logically to one of the goals. They should also be challenging but achievable. Multiple means of measurement may be used to measure an objective, especially complex objectives that may have more than one dimension.

Including both goals and objectives in a strategic plan helps those developing the plan to go from the big picture (mission and vision), to important outcomes (goals), to measurable indicators of accomplishment (objectives). This is an important thought progression.

Goals

Goals are broad statements of intent. Goals are the broad "brush strokes" that point the organization in a general strategic direction as articulated in the organization's mission and vision statements, but do not provide the detail necessary to hold people accountable for achievement. While goals are expressed in general, high-level terms, they include those activities which are most likely to impact the performance of the institution. In other words, goals outline the relatively few things that must go right if the institution is to flourish. For example, the statement, "to become the educational institution of choice for public accounting firms in Southern California" is a goal that reflects intention, and thus has the potential to be a good goal. But stating the goal immediately raises important questions, such as, "how will we know that we have accomplished this goal," and "what is the time period for accomplishing the goal," and "how are we going to do this?" The same is true for the goal, "to grow our degree completion programs in psychology at our regional locations." Stating the goal leads to asking important questions that are answered in the process of developing objectives, strategies, and action plans.

Objectives

As mentioned earlier, objectives are specific desired outcomes or performance targets, stated in measurable language. For each goal in the strategic plan, at least one objective is needed, and some goals will require multiple objectives.

For an objective to be a good objective, and thus provide direction and a standard for evaluation, it should be a SMART objective. A SMART objective is:

Specific

Measurable

Achievable

Relevant

Time-based

Let's examine each of these criteria, including an example of a poorly-written objective and one that is better.

Specific. Objectives should be written, and they should be clear and concise. There should not be any room for misunderstanding in what results are sought in a given objective. Avoid the use of long statements with words or phrases which may be defined or interpreted in different ways by different people.

Poor: To be the best university in the state.

This objective lacks specificity. What does it mean to be the "best university"? Is being the best based on size? Reputation? Programs? Graduation rate? Faculty publications?

Better: To have the highest student placement rate of any private university in the state.

This is better, although the metrics for determining student placement rates would need to be determined so that progress toward accomplishment can be monitored.

Measurable. A good objective contains criteria for assessing progress so that results can be compared against a standard. Measuring progress helps people to stay on track, accomplish results, and experience the exhilaration that comes from accomplishing important objectives.

Poor: To maximize student learning.

While every university hopes to maximize student learning, there has to be some way of assessing that learning. What level of student learning would constitute maximizing student learning?

Better: To achieve learning outcomes such that 90 percent of graduates will pass the state licensure examination on the first attempt.

Achievable. Objectives should be challenging but attainable. Challenging goals provide motivation and stimulate effort, but unattainable goals produce frustration. Balance is required in this area. There are times when creating stretch objectives, which require accomplishment beyond what is considered possible by those involved, can be a good thing—especially when it works. On the other hand, creating totally unrealistic objectives is likely to produce zero motivation, and is thus not recommended.

Poor: To achieve a 100 percent pass rate on the CPA exam on the first try within six months of graduation for all CPA-track accounting majors.

This objective is specific and measurable, but is probably not attainable. CPA pass rates have hovered around 50 percent for the last several years, and the percentage of those who pass on the first try is lower.[33] And aiming at 100 percent means that if anyone does not take the exam, or has a bad day, the objective will not be reached.

Better: To achieve a 60 percent pass rate on each section of the CPA exam within nine months of graduation for all CPA-track accounting majors.

Whether this specific objective is the correct pass rate would depend on your institution's history and prior results. For example, if your pass rate is currently at 35

---

[33]https://www.aicpa.org/BecomeACPA/CPAExam/PsychometricsandScoring/PassingRates/DownloadableDocuments/Pass-Rates-2016.pdf

percent, then achieving 60 percent in a year is unlikely. Perhaps a challenging, yet realistic objective would be to consistently increase the pass rate five percent each year for the next five years, bringing the pass rate up to 60 percent by the end of that period of time.

Relevant. It is important that objectives be relevant. Generally, this means that each objective should be consistent with the university's mission, vision, and goals. This seems obvious, but can be a problem in any organization, including academic ones. Universities are full of gifted faculty members who have become specialists in specific (and sometimes arcane) areas. Sometimes these individuals seek to create programs that cater to their particular interests but are not of interest to enough other people to be viable programs. The strategic planning process can become a place where individuals try to write their idiosyncratic desires into organizational reality. It is important, therefore, to examine all objectives for relevance with the university's mission, vision, and goals. Insisting up front that all objectives be relevant provides a good way to say no to things that the university should not be doing.

Poor. To develop a world-class program in nuclear science in the next five years.

There are a few universities for whom this would be a relevant objective, but let's assume you work at a small college with strengths in the liberal arts. Nuclear science is not relevant to the mission and vision of your university, so this would not be a good objective for your institution.

Better: To develop a world-class program is English as a Second Language in the next five years.

For the small liberal arts college, this is probably a better objective, although whether there is the potential for competitive advantage in this area is a good question, as is the five-year time frame.

Time-Based. Objectives should be stated for a specific time period. Objectives can be set for a short run, or an immediate time period such as six months to one year. Building on longer time frames, accomplishment of short-term objectives should serve as segments of a successful completion of longer-term objectives. The time period specified becomes a deadline for producing results, and also sets up the final evaluation of the success of a strategy. The time period specified in an objective provide an important input into action planning, as will be discussed in the next chapter.

Poor: To increase contributions of first-time givers.

This objective is not measurable, in that it does not specify a target for the increased contributions. It also is not time-based, since it does not specify a time period. Therefore, if contributions of first-time givers increase by a total of $50 over five years, the objective has been met. But that's probably not the intent.

Better: To increase donations from first-time givers by 10 percent each year over the next three years.

This objective is now both measurable and time-based, thus making assessment of accomplishment possible.

Challenges in Setting Objectives

Writing good objectives is not easy, especially if it is clear that all objectives must be SMART objectives. But there are a few other challenges that should be noted.

Focusing on what is easy to accomplish rather than what is important. Easy goals are easy to accomplish, and can create an illusion of accomplishment. This results in performance evaluations that look good from a distance—since every goal is being accomplished— but camouflage lackluster performance well short of the potential.

Focusing on what is easy to measure rather than what is important. Requiring that objectives be specific, measurable, and time-based can lead people to write objectives for which data is easily available, rather than writing objectives that lead to accomplishment of key goals.

Focusing on what is easy to fund rather than what is important. Resources are an important constraint in any organization, given that the foundational concept of economics is unlimited wants but limited resources. There are many great ideas that have been discarded because funding was not immediately available. Sometimes that is necessary. But good ideas should not be summarily dismissed based only on funding constraints. If something is really worth doing, there's at least some chance that funding can be raised for it.

Focusing on what has been funded rather than on what leads to competitive advantage. When donors make funding available for programs, often universities fail to ask whether the program is something that leads to competitive advantage and is, therefore, something they ought to be doing. This can lead to a lack of strategic focus.

Focusing on the past rather than the future. In universities, it is typically far easier to start a program than to end one. And, especially in institutions with tenure, shutting down a program can be a lengthy and expensive process. Individuals will often try to protect themselves and their programs in the strategic planning process. But the concept of creating and sustaining competitive advantage is, by its nature, a process that looks to the future.

Next Steps

In this chapter, we have discussed mission, vision, key result areas, goals, and objectives. Mission and vision help to answer the "why" question; goals and objectives help to answer the "what" question. In the next chapter, we will begin to answer the "how" question by discussing strategies and action plans.

8
DEVELOPING A STRATEGIC PLAN: STRATEGIES AND ACTION PLANS

Knowing *what* you need to accomplish strategically, and *why* you need to do so, is essential. Determining *how* may be even more important, and this is where developing strategies and action plans is important. As tempting as it may be to assume that objectives will accomplish themselves, that's not reality.

A strategy is a method for accomplishing an objective. In a larger sense, a strategy is a method for bringing about a desired future. In business, there are several categories of strategies, some of which may be helpful in determining how to reach your objectives, so we will look at some of those strategies in this chapter. In many cases, however, good people doing good thinking develop good strategies. In other words, brainstorming is an essential tool for strategy development.

Strategies come in all sizes. Corporate-level or "grand" strategies look at the overall direction of an organization; "business-level" strategies look at how a particular business unit attempts to compete in its industry; and "functional-level" strategies focus at the departmental level. In a private university, the business-level and functional-level strategies are the most used in a strategic plan.

The GE/McKinsey strategy matrix can be helpful in thinking about the overall direction of your university. Begin by thinking about the ways in which your university competes in the marketplace. One way to do this is by thinking about the major student groups that you target. For example, most private IHEs serve traditional residential students, and that group is a substantial portion of the total student body. You may also be serving non-traditional students through face-to-face or online modalities, and those students are a substantial portion of your student body. Because of the differences in serving these different groups of students and the ways in which your university is structured to serve them, you may be, in essence, competing in two different industries. For the sake of example (and at the risk of oversimplification), let's call these two groups Trad and Nontrad.

The GE/McKinsey matrix examines market attractiveness and business strength, as shown in Table 2. To use the model, you would analyze the attractiveness of the markets in which your Trad and Nontrad units compete. Market attractiveness is influenced by market size, market growth rate, average profitability of the market, and intensity of competition. Note that market attractiveness is an external variable; these are all factors that are external to your institution.

Business strength, on the other hand, is internal. Business strength looks at how strong of a competitor are you in the marketplace. Business strength is influenced by market share, market share growth rate, product quality, brand reputation, promotional effectiveness, and innovative capacity.

Because you compete in different markets and with different units of your university, the market attractiveness and business strength will typically vary among your Trad and Nontrad units. For example, given trends in enrollment for traditional students mentioned earlier in this book, it is likely that market attractiveness will be lower for Trad than for Nontrad.

Once you have determined market attractiveness and business strength for the Trad and Nontrad units, you can look at the strategies suggested by the model for each of these units. If the unit falls into the cells in the upper-left corner of the model, growth strategies are suggested. If the unit falls into the cells in the lower-right corner of the model, retrenchment strategies are suggested. In the middle, selective strategies are suggested.

Please note that we use the word "suggested." This model is designed to help strategy-makers think through the situation, and that can be very helpful. If a unit of a university is in a market with limited attractiveness and has low business strength, an aggressive growth strategy is highly unlikely to work.

Table 2

GE/McKinsey Matrix

		Business Strength		
		Strong	Medium	Weak
Market Attractiveness	High	**Protect Position** • Invest to grow at maximum digestible rate • Concentrate effort on maintaining strength	**Invest to Build** • Challenge for leadership • Build selectively on strengths • Reinforce vulnerable areas	**Build Selectively** • Specialize around limited strengths • Seek ways to overcome weaknesses • Withdraw if indications of sustainable growth are lacking
	Medium	**Build Selectively** • Invest heavily in most attractive segments • Build up ability to counter competition • Emphasize profitability by raising productivity	**Selectivity/Manage for Earnings** • Protect existing program • Concentrate investments in segments where profitability is good and risks are relatively low	**Limited Expansion or Harvest** • Look for ways to expand without high risk; otherwise minimize investments and rationalize operations
	Low	**Protect and Refocus** • Manage for current earnings • Concentrate on attractive segments • Defend strengths	**Manage for Earnings** • Protect position in most profitable segments • Upgrade product line • minimize investment	**Divest** • Sell at time that will maximize cash value • Cut fixed costs and avoid investment meanwhile

Another useful way to think about business-level strategy is Miles and Snow's Strategy Typology,[34] which suggests that there are four different types of organizations. Prospectors innovate, find new market opportunities, take risks, and focus on growth. Defenders protect their turf and attempt to hold onto their current market. Analyzers hold their current market, but also innovate around the edges of that market. And Reactors drift, with no clearly discernable strategy. Miles and Snow suggested that these different types of organizations operate in different environments and tend to have different organizational characteristics, and shown in Table 3.

[34] Miles, R.E., Snow, C.C, Meyer, A.D., & Coleman, Jr., H.L. (1978). Organizational strategy, structure, and process. *Academy of Management Review*, 3, 546-562.

Table 3

Miles and Snow's Strategy Typology

	Strategy	**Environment**	**Organizational Characteristics**
Prospector	Innovates, grows, finds new market opportunities, takes risks	Dynamic, growing	Creative, innovative, flexible, decentralized
Defender	Protects turf, holds current market, retrenches	Stable	Tight control, centralized, low overhead
Analyzer	Maintains position in main market, plus innovates in related markets	Moderately changing	Combines tight control and flexibility, creativity
Reactor	No clear strategy, reacts to changing conditions, drifts	Can be any environment	No clear organizational approach; varies depending on current needs

The best strategy depends on the environment in which your university operates and on its capabilities. A reactor strategy, however, is likely to fail regardless of the situation, and is therefore not recommended.

A Hypothetical Example

Let's assume your institution is a medium-size private university located in the Los Angeles metro area. Your music programs at both the undergraduate and graduate levels are outstanding, as is your theatre program. You have significant connections with the entertainment industry, and substantial numbers of alumni employed in the entertainment industry in a wide variety of positions. You also have significant strengths in business, with strong undergraduate and graduate programs and a highly-regarded "shark tank" competition and a fairly new business incubator.

Given these characteristics, you determine that you should be able to develop a competitive advantage in preparing students for various careers in the entertainment industry. Thus you develop the following objective:

Objective 1: Within seven years, place 150 students in positions in the entertainment industry.

By this point, you have analyzed the external environment, determined strengths and weaknesses of your university, and considered the potential for developing a competitive advantage. And you have written a SMART objective. You have thought about the why and the what, so now the question becomes, "how?" What strategies will you use to attempt to accomplish this objective? In terms of the GE/McKinsey matrix, you have determined that a moderately attractive market opportunity exists and that your institution has significant strengths to pursue that opportunity, and thus can follow a somewhat assertive strategy. In terms of the Miles and Snow typology, you are becoming an Analyzer by innovating at the edges of the existing organization.

Several components of your university's supply chain—such as enrollment management, admissions, academics, career services, and alumni services—would need to become involved in this initiative, with strategies needed in each area. For example, the following strategies (among others) might be created.

Strategy 1: Develop an undergraduate degree program in music entrepreneurship with courses provided by both the school of music and the school of business.

Strategy 2: Create an entertainment industry advisory board composed of both alumni and non-alumni.

Strategy 3: Develop entertainment industry internships.

Note that these strategies begin to show how your organization will accomplish the objective of placing 150 students in positions in the entertainment industry in seven year. These strategies, however, do not contain the level of detail needed for implementation. That's where action planning comes in.

Action Planning

To implement a strategy requires an action plan. The action plan details the steps and processes necessary to implement the strategy. It indicates the person or persons with primary responsibility for each step, determines whose approval or support is necessary, provides deadlines for each step, and estimates the relevant costs. A table or spreadsheet can be helpful in portraying the action plan, as shown below:

Objective 1: Within seven years, place 150 students in positions in the entertainment industry.

Strategy 2: Create an entertainment industry advisory board composed of both alumni and non-alumni.

Action Plan	Person(s) with Primary Responsibility	Required Support/ Approval	Deadline	Relevant Costs
Meet with advancement office to discuss entertainment industry connections	Music dean	Advancement office Academic affairs	April 30	
Meet with alumni office to discuss alumni in entertainment industry	Music dean	Alumni office Academic affairs	May 15	
Brainstorm entertainment industry connections with faculty	Music dean, chairs		May 30	$200 for snacks
Develop advisory board expectations document	Music dean	Alumni office	June 30	
Announce in alumni newsletter	Newsletter coordinator	Music dean	July 30	
Develop list of potential members	Music dean, chairs, faculty	Advancement office	August 30	
Post announcement and application in alumni newsletter	Newsletter coordinator	Alumni office	August 30	

This chapter has examined how to develop strategies and actions plans, which is the final part of the process of developing a strategic plan. We have included an outline of a strategic plan in the Appendix. The final chapter examines strategic execution, which is essential to getting strategy right.

9
GETTING IT RIGHT:
STRATEGIC EXECUTION

The relationship between strategy and its execution is much like the two sides of a coin. Yes, they are two separate things, but it is impossible to tell where the front and back sides of the coin begin and end. If the coin is flipped, it is equally likely that either side will land face up. So it is with strategy and execution. Done well, it is impossible to see where the strategy ends and the execution begins. Done poorly, execution exists apart from strategic thinking and planning. This results in a dangerous situation where the university is susceptible to dramatic changes in the market. Because organizational efforts are not aligned with its strategic plans, the university cannot execute well, and the result is a negative impact on enrollment.

Let's look at a generic example. XYZ University is scheduled for its 10th-year comprehensive accreditation visit from its regional accreditor. Approximately 18 months in advance of the visit, the campus hurriedly assembles a writing team to draft the self-study document. As a part of the self-study, the writing team includes a campus strategic plan, various metrics on budget and enrollment figures, and several chapters of evidence that purport to show that the university has met the criteria for accreditation. Massive amounts of communication occur to the campus community in the weeks leading up to the visit to remind everyone of the campus mission statement and the various elements of the "good story" that is XYZ University. The visiting team arrives and conducts its assessment of the university. The team leaves after a few days, and—assuming a positive outcome—much rejoicing is heard that the university has been re-accredited for another ten years.

This is where the mistake happens.

All of the momentum gained over the past 18 months will be wasted if the planning documents created as a part of the self-study are simply filed away for another 8-½ years until it's time to prepare for the next accreditation visit. The worst strategic plan is the one that is created just for show and ceases to influence any unit's behavior on campus as soon as the visiting team leaves. To enjoy exceptional returns, it is absolutely critical that mission, strategy, and execution be in alignment.

Whether you are a faculty member leading a committee, a dean leading an academic school, a provost leading the entire academic structure, or a president leading an entire institution, it is imperative to remember that your people are your greatest resource in achieving the goals you seek. It isn't necessary to reinvent the wheel when focusing on the execution of your carefully constructed strategic plan. Much has already been written about successful execution of strategy. We have condensed them here as a set of best practices in execution that be readily adapted to aid you in the execution of your plans. What follows, then, are our recommendations as to how to adapt these disciplines to a private higher education setting.

Focus on what's really important.[35] The most common strategic derailleur is to lose sight of what you are really trying to accomplish. That is, to focus on the urgent at the expense of the important. As academic administrators, it is all too easy to have your calendar filled with those decisions and conversations that, while urgent, provide little if any momentum toward the achievement of your goals. For example, if your strategic plans calls for your campus to increase its enrollment by five percent via the establishment of three new masters-level programs, then getting those three programs created, approved, and deployed must be top of mind. Let's assume that the provost is the responsible party in this scenario. The provost likely will generate a list of action plan steps in order to accomplish this objective that might include:

- Meet with respective deans and faculty members to gain buy-in on the development of these graduate programs.
- Negotiate load release time for faculty to develop the academic components of the degrees.

---

[35] McChesney, C., Covey, S., & Huling, J. (2012). *The 4 disciplines of execution.* NY: The Free Press.

- Work with each dean to create a needs assessment for each program
- Work with VP of Enrollment to develop an enrollment projection for each program
- Work with VP of Business/Finance to establish a budget for each program
- Schedule academic proposals to be heard before faculty approval committee(s)
- Seek cabinet and/or board approvals for each new program (if necessary)
- Complete paperwork and seek approval from regional accrediting body
- Seek approval from the specialized accrediting body that governs the respective academic areas (if such accreditation is present)

Short-term projects of this type are nothing new to academic administrators; they are simply part of the job. However, the tyranny of the urgent needs of day-to-day activities act to slow down or stop entirely our progress toward the accomplishment of this initiative. Phone calls, emails, unexpected faculty/staff vacancies in key areas, fundraising, day-to-day staff management, grade appeals, community involvement, and a hundred other activities can overwhelm even the best administrator if not managed intentionally and closely. Keep your focus on the goal and resist the urge to become sidetracked.

Act on Leading Measures.[36] Once established, a strategic objective must drive the parties responsible for its accomplishment to reinvent the way they manage. Flowing from your focus on what's really important, you must prioritize the activities that drive accomplishment rather than focusing on lagging measures. Continuing with our example of increasing enrollment by developing new graduate programs, student enrollment is not only the lagging measure, but also the ultimate goal. Success will be driven by acting on the activities that make it possible to open these new programs. Thus, ignore enrollment figures. Focus your efforts on the near-term activities it takes to develop the program, budget the program, staff the program, and approve the program internally and externally. Only then can you shift your focus to recruitment for the program.

Keep a compelling scorecard.[37] If a campus makes a mistake with data, it's usually one of extremes. At one extreme, execution efforts can be undermined by simply having no data whatsoever; thus, no one knows whether or to what extent objectives have been achieved. On the other extreme, a campus will publish an annual "data book" of some type that details all the critical demographic details of their student body; a superfluous amount of data. It's tempting to use this publication in its entirety as a set of trackable metrics as you execute your plan. The key advice here is to avoid overwhelming your team with massive amounts of data. It doesn't take much data to keep your team members informed and equipped with the strategic information they need to maintain momentum.

---

[36] McChesney, C., Covey, S., & Huling, J. (2012). *The 4 disciplines of execution.* NY: The Free Press.
[37] Ibid.

An idea from corporate America that has only recently begun to penetrate the higher education industry is the use of a balanced scorecard. The idea is fairly simplistic. Develop a "digital dashboard" containing the metrics that objectively measure progress toward a strategic goal or objective. Just as the dashboard on a car shows a real-time status of the car's systems that are most critical to the driver, the balanced scorecard should be updated constantly (or as often as the metrics change) with the information that are most critical to its users. For example, suppose your university has a strategic goal of reducing its tuition discount rate for athletes. The people most interested in this would be the VP of Enrollment, the Director of Financial Aid, the Director of the Business Office, the Athletic Director, and the coaches of the individual sports. A balanced scorecard would most likely include the annual amount budgeted for institutional aid broken out by team (or coach), the percent of each team's scholarship budget that is appropriated, student headcount per team, other institutional aid (such as academic scholarships), net tuition revenue per player, etc.

Develop a solid value proposition.[38] We know a university president who has a familiar phrase he uses often with his team, "Stay on mission. Stay on message." That's good advice. To communicate the inherent value of those long-term capabilities you are building into your value chain, your campus needs to speak with one voice to its constituencies. This strategy is built upon the realization that the majority of listeners are listening passively, rather than actively, thus

---

[38] Chan, K., & Mauborgne, R. (February 5, 2015). Closing the gap between blue ocean strategy and execution. *Harvard Business Review.*

requiring repetition of the message. In his book, *Leading Change*, John Kotter of the Harvard Business School wrote that many change efforts fail "...because of the under-communication of the vision by a factor of 10, 100, or 1000."[39] That all-important value proposition becomes the talking point about your campus or your program. Don't be discouraged when your constituencies (students, parents, donors, community members, faculty members, etc.) roll their eyes when you state your value proposition in a speech, article, or message. When they do, you should take it as a signal that you are just beginning to get through to them about the value proposition of your campus. Use your value proposition in advertising messages and campus communications of all types—both internally and externally. Remember that your internal constituencies need to hear this message as much as your external constituencies do, because they will, in turn, carry your message into their circle of influence.

Create a culture of ongoing accountability.[40] Results don't just happen by accident. People will focus on whatever is measured. Therefore, it will not be sufficient to focus on top-down accountability. Rather, you must focus on accountability at all levels where change is taking place. Remember that compelling scorecard we spoke about earlier? Put it to use. Administrators, faculty, and staff members alike must be equipped with the scorecard and held accountable for their respective role in the successes or failures in the changes. If you have defined the data correctly and connected it

---

[39] Kotter, J. (2012). *Leading Change*. Boston, MA: Harvard Business Review Press.
[40] McChesney, C., Covey, S., & Huling, J. (2012). *The 4 disciplines of execution*. NY: The Free Press.

responsibly to everyone's position, no one will be (or should be) surprised at the outcome. A word of warning, however, is necessary when managing with data. Don't mistake communication for understanding, and don't mistake understanding for mastery. Temper your expectations about the pace of change with the knowledge that the members of your team will need time to translate your visionary strategic message into an understanding of its applications. Likewise, once understanding is achieved, they will need time to develop a mastery of the new knowledge, skills, and abilities they must develop.

Let strategy drive structural change—always. We encourage you to resist the temptation to allow the status quo to drive the change process. In all likelihood, the strategies you've developed will fly in the face of the status quo, and in so doing will threaten the established power and resource relationships within the organization. The formula for success isn't difficult to design, but it is difficult to hold together. The formula is to develop good strategies, design proper structures, staff them with excellent people, fund them appropriately, and demand accountability. Misalignment of these resources, that is, to allow mission, strategy, and structure to come out of alignment, will guarantee that you fail to meet your objective measures of success.

Cut costs and make targeted investments.[41] By far the most common strategic mistake campuses make is not at the

---

[41] Leinwand, P., Mainardi, C., & Kleiner, A. (December, 2015). Only 8% of Leaders are Good at Both Strategy and Execution. *Harvard Business Review*.

beginning of the strategic planning process, it's at the end. Too often, academic administrators (under the guise of being altruistic) will hang on too long to programs (and the faculty and staff members that support them) that don't sell or bring in new student revenues. In many cases, a campus will have multiple degree programs that are underenrolled and should be significantly revised or closed. A strong system of program review should be in place on every campus. This should include not just a review of academic programs, but also of administrative programs and services that have outlived their usefulness. This review process will ultimately free up badly needed fiscal resources that can then be used to make targeted investments into new programs that provide a much higher growth potential. While this review process can sound harsh or scary to faculty members and administrators alike, it is not healthy to avoid the process. The result of this process does not always mean the loss of personnel. However, in almost every case, it results in a cost savings of some type. Often, this resource becomes your first round of institutional investment for new strategic plans.

Walk and speak boldly and with confidence. When speaking of strategic planning, one of the authors of this text is fond of saying, "Build your plan, have your plan, work your plan, trust your plan." It is this last point that is pertinent here. It is common that the processes described in this text may take several years to come to fruition. During this period, the demands placed upon leadership will be great in order to communicate the plan effectively, overcome objections, make hard decisions, and demand accountability. Don't be dismayed if some on your team lose heart or need constant reassurance. Trust the plan you've created. You will accomplish much more by following the plan than if you just tell people to "go do your best" without sufficient direction or accountability. Walk boldly and speak with confidence.

Get help. Finally, if you need help, get help! Developing an understanding of your institution's competitive advantages and value proposition can take time, and there are many potential pitfalls and roadblocks along the way. It is likely that at least one of your business professors is very familiar with these concepts, and could provide leadership in the process. It is amazing how few institutions are willing to include the strategy professor in the strategic planning process!

There are times, however, when an expert from the outside can help the institution walk through challenging parts of the process, and thus navigate the pitfalls and roadblocks more successfully. If needed, we stand ready to help your institution as it develops its competitive advantage and crafts a winning strategy.

For Further Reading

Leinwand, P., Mainardi, C., & Kleiner, A. (December, 2015). 5 ways to close the strategy-to-execution gap. *Harvard Business Review.*

Leinwand, P., Mainardi, C., & Kleiner, A. (December, 2015). Only 8% of leaders are good at both strategy and execution. *Harvard Business Review.*

McChesney, C., Covey, S., & Huling, J. (2012). *The 4 disciplines of execution.* NY: The Free Press.

Neilson, G., Martin, K., & Powers, E. (June, 2008). The secrets to successful strategy execution. *Harvard Business Review.*

Trevor, J., & Varcoe, B. (May 2016). A simple way to test your company's strategic alignment. *Harvard Business Review.*

Chan, K., & Mauborgne, R. (February 5, 2015). Closing the gap between blue ocean strategy and execution. *Harvard Business Review.*

APPENDIX

COMPONENTS OF A STRATEGIC PLAN
FOR A UNIVERSITY

Strategic Plan Components

Organizational Profile

- History
- Mission
- Vision
- Foundational assumptions
- Guiding values
- Key stakeholders

Internal analysis

- Strengths
- Weaknesses
- Analysis of competitive advantage (VRIO)
- Value proposition

External analysis

- Sociological trends
- Technological trends
- Economic trends
- Political trends
- Industry analysis/attractiveness
- Summary of opportunities and threats

Key result areas

Goals

Objectives

Strategies

Action plans

ABOUT THE AUTHORS

Brett K. Andrews, MBA, Ph.D. currently serves as the Dean for the School of Business at Newman University. As an author, speaker, coach, executive, and consultant, he has a passion for helping universities achieve growth and significance through outstanding leadership, new revenue development, and campus strategy development. His 20+ year career in private Christian higher education has given him a well-rounded background in creating partnerships and alliances between campuses and corporations. Recognized as a thought leader for go-to-market models with new academic programs, he is a regular contributor to and speaker at public forums and conferences.

Robert H. Roller, MBA, Ph.D. brings a passion for cultivating difference makers into everything he does in his role as the Dean for the School of Business and Management at Azusa Pacific University. Dr. Roller is an experienced academic leader and an expert in faith-learning integration, business accreditation, continuous quality improvement in education, and strategic planning. An experienced president and dean, Dr. Roller has spoken at conferences and workshops and consulted with educational institutions throughout the world. He has authored many journal publications and made numerous presentations at regional, national, and international meetings.

R. Henry Migliore, Ph.D. – Has led a life dedicated to helping others succeed. He works with a wide range of hospital, government, athletic, profit, and nonprofit organizations. A former School of Business Dean, his primary role has been strategic planning, problem solving, and team building for action and solutions. Dr. Migliore's formula for developing supportive functional plans and their coordination with the organization's overall strategic plan is unique. He is the author of 17 books on the subject of strategy that have been translated into 7 languages.

50998807R00078

Made in the USA
San Bernardino, CA
10 July 2017